# Monster Mysteries

# MONSTER MYSTERIES

## John Grant

Grange
BOOKS

A QUINTET BOOK

Published by Grange Books
An imprint of Grange Books plc
The Grange
Grange Yard
London SE1 3AG

This edition published 1995

ISBN 1-85627-811-5

This book was designed and produced by
Quintet Publishing Limited
6 Blundell Street
London N7 9BH

Creative Director: Richard Dewing
Designer: Nicky Chapman
Project Editor: Laura Sandelson
Editor: Lydia Darbyshire
Picture Researcher: Jill De Cet

Typeset in Great Britain by
Central Southern Typesetters, Eastbourne
Manufactured in China by
Regent Publishing Services Limited
Printed in Singapore by
Star Standard Industries (Pte) Ltd

# CONTENTS

# INTRODUCTION

Monster-hunters are fond of quoting Sherlock Holmes's dictum that "when you have eliminated the impossible, whatever remains, *however improbable*, must be the truth". In the wrong hands this is, of course, as dangerous a maxim as the dismissive "There are more things in heaven and earth, Horatio, than are dreamt of in your philosophy", which allows all sorts of cranks and crackpots to attribute the most unlikely interpretations to perfectly mundane, if as yet not wholly explained, phenomena. There is always a danger, in acknowledging that there are still many things that lie beyond the accepted corpus of human knowledge, of going too far the other way, of accepting as fact things that are really only rumours or popular beliefs or of adopting explanations that are attractively imaginative rather than boringly true. Our ideal when dealing with subjects such as monsters is to be open-minded. Most of the crackpots give lip-service to this idea while, in fact, being as close-minded as any of the orthodox scientists whom they abuse, and this comment applies also to some quite genuine researchers into what we might call fringe knowledge.

Yet Holmes had a point. There does come a time when the evidence in favour of some conclusion or another becomes overwhelming – even if you do not much *like* the conclusion concerned, it would be perverse not to admit its likelihood. An example that is discussed in this book concerns the large wildcats that have been reported quite consistently over the years in Britain: there may be a perfectly mundane explanation for their existence – they could be the descendants of zoo escapees, for example – or they may indeed represent an unknown species. Whatever the truth of the matter, consigning the cats to the dustbins of folklore would be to commit an extremely unscientific error, especially since examples of at least one of their varieties, the Kellas cats of Scotland, have been shot and examined.

In other scenarios it is certainly the case that it would be as foolish to reject the possibility that a particular monster exists as to embrace its existence wholeheartedly. In such instances, we have to agree with the other favourite maxim of the monster-hunter – that there is just too much evidence for something to be as glibly dismissed as it usually is. To choose one exposition of this point from an abundance, let me quote the zoologist Karl P. N. Shuker, who, after quoting Holmes, sums up his excellent *Mystery Cats of the World* thus:

After having eliminated the impossible relative to mystery cats – viz. that *all* reports of *all* such creatures result from dimly viewed dogs, manic mendacity, drunken delusion or mass hallucination – we are left with an initially improbable but ultimately inevitable conclusion: namely, that mystery cats of wide diversity and worldwide distribution do exist.

John Napier says much the same of the North American Bigfoot. Bernard Heuvelmans says it of both the Yeti and the sea-serpents. It is hardly irrational to agree with the validity of their argument: there is *something* there, even if it may not prove to be exactly what the researchers think it is. Unfortunately, a very similar line of argument is imitated by innumerable less rigorous researchers about their own monsters, which we can describe generically as the Mysterious Bugbear; and it is used to less honourable ends – to "prove beyond doubt" not just that there must be something in these tales of Bugbears, not just that the Bugbear exists, but that it is *the exact very same Bugbear, down to the minutiae of its unsavoury habits, that the author states it to be*. Of course, the argument cannot be taken to prove anything of the sort. We might similarly "prove" that all Martians are green – have you ever seen anyone green who *isn't* a Martian? – with equally fallacious results.

How, then, can we evaluate the monsters described in the pages of this book? We might imagine that there was some sort of a "probability scale", with a score of 10 implying that something was known for certain to exist and a score of zero for something that certainly does not. For my own part, I would be prepared to award a few of these monsters a 10 – the cats mentioned above, for example – and some of them maybe a nine (indicating that I would be somewhat surprised to find that they *did not* exist), but, as for the others, I would not like to be tied down. Certainly I would have no confidence in bestowing a zero on any of them. So, although you will find in places that I have reached tentative conclusions as to the likelihood or (more frequently) otherwise of a reported monster being what it claims to be, in the event the judgement has to be yours . . . if, and here is another moot question, it makes any sense to apply something like judgement to such matters, for we can all "judge" away to our hearts' contents and it makes not one whit of difference to whether or not a specific monster is genuine.

In other words, we must try to attain that ideal of being truly open-minded while at the same time remembering the pitfall of having an open mind: people come along and put things in it.　　　　　J. G.

ABOVE An artist's impression of the North American Bigfoot. It would seem that the artist has been influenced by our ideas of prehistoric Man.

# CHAPTER ONE

# BIGFOOT

The possibility that there may be alive in the world today a human-sized and humanoid creature, possessed of at least the intelligence of a chimpanzee, might seem to be a remote one, but tales of such beings are found in a remarkable number of widely separated cultures, notably through much of Asia and North America and to a lesser extent elsewhere. Similar tales were treated as moonshine by European explorers in Africa until, in the middle of the 19th century, science was forced to recognize the existence of the gorilla, which until then had been dismissed as a folkloric "wild man of the woods". This is by no means an isolated example of science – or, rather, of scientists – having refused to pay attention to copiously repeated anecdotal evidence that did not fit in with science's accepted worldview; and pseudoscientists have frequently picked upon such examples to support their varyingly madcap theses, on the basis that, if the scientists were wrong about this and this and *this*, their refusal to believe that the Earth is hollow is just because they are bigoted, ignorant, narrow-minded, locked in the ivory towers of academe, terrified for their reputations and so on. In fact, modern scientists have it right a depressingly large fraction of the time: the point of citing the example of the gorilla is that the fact that we have little evidence for the existence of large humanoid animals apart from the anecdotal is not in itself sufficient reason for dismissing the possibility of their existence out of hand.

Different cultures have different names for their own version of the wild man. In this discussion we will (usually) make the fairly daring assumption that all of these types of wild men are of the same species, perhaps varying in precise detail from region to region of the world to the same extent that members of the species *Homo sapiens* do – which is to say, barely at all. The assumption, although widely made, is unjustifiable, of course; we have adopted it primarily for conveninece. Similarly for convenience, we use the generic term Bigfoot for all varieties except when there is particular reason to be more specific, even though, strictly speaking, by Bigfoot we should refer only to the wild man of North America. Since, in this stricter usage, the terms Sasquatch and Bigfoot are virtually synonymous, we shall generally talk of the Sasquatch when

RIGHT The character of Harry in Harry and the Hendersons has erroneously led people to believe Bigfoot is sometimes cute and friendly.

RIGHT A man's foot compared with a plastercast made of a footprint discovered after the famous sighting and filming of Bigfoot by Roger Patterson in 1967.

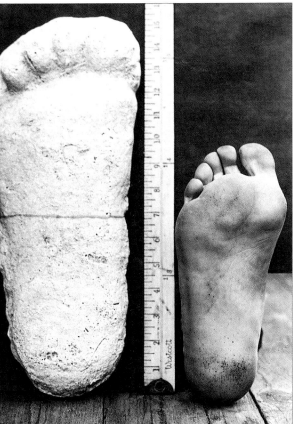

concerned with North America. The wild man of Asia, notably of the Himalayas, is generally known as the Yeti or the Abominable Snowman. Another important grouping of legends covers the territories of the former Soviet Union, and of Mongolia and China: here the wild man is called the Alma.

Thanks to the entertainment media, our popular perceptions of Bigfoot are muddled. Children may thrill to the thought that Bigfoot is implacably hostile and murderous or that the creature is cute and friendly, like the hero of *Harry and the Hendersons*, yet many – far from all – of the traditions contradict both of these impressions. They report that Bigfoot is shy and frightened of human beings, which probably explains its habit of residing only in the most remote parts of the world, avoiding as far as possible any contact with its destructive sister species. Another popular misconception is that Bigfoot is huge; again, the various direct-encounter reports, when collated, show that the average estimated height is 1.5–1.8m (5–6ft) and sometimes much shorter. One can suggest that Bigfoot is probably somewhat shorter than a normal adult human because observers will naturally tend to exaggerate the size of the "monsters" they have encountered. (Moreover, size and height are not the same thing. Gorillas are not tall compared with ourselves, but they are big.) This matter of stature is important, because a prevalent theory to explain Bigfoot is that these creatures are the scattered remnants of Neanderthal Man, *Homo neanderthalis*, or possibly just a subspecies of *Homo sapiens*, a form of hominid generally believed to have become extinct about 35,000 years ago when the more aggressive Cro-Magnon Man, our ancestor, came into the ascendant. It would seem not unreasonable that the timid, persecuted Neanderthals might retreat to those remote regions whose inhospitability would make it not worth the Cro-Magnons' while to compete for. However, this theory is purely specula-tion, since earlier pictures of the Cro-Magnons exterminating the Neanderthals seem, in the light of modern knowledge, simplistic – indeed, the two varieties jof hominid appear to have coexisted and cooperated quite happily, at least in some parts of the world. Another point is that we have no particular reason to believe that the Neander-thals were especially hairy, whereas reports of Bigfoot are almost unanimous on this.

A different possibility is that Bigfoot is an ape. It is perfectly reason-able to think that some of the known varieties of apes may have a wider range of habitats than we currently suppose. Moreover, there may be varieties of apes of which science as yet knows nothing, with the gorilla a century and a half ago. It might seem incredible that – armed with much more sophisticated detection equipment and substantially better communications, and exploring a wilderness whose extent has substantially diminished as our technological civilization has eroded away more and more of it – modern science could have such a large lacuna in its knowledge, but this is to forget quite how wild and inaccessible the remaining wilderness can be. Moreover, it was not too terribly long ago that zoologists were proclaiming that every decent-sized mammal in the world was now known to them: nature shortly thereafter yielded up the okapi, which is about the size of a horse.

## THE EVIDENCE

If we cannot say for certain that Bigfoot does *not* exist, what evidence do we have to show that it does? The immediate answer is: not much. Photographs abound, of course, but there has been a deal of hoaxing, and, while most of the fakes are crude and readily discredited, some of the more sophisticated fabrications are hard to detect. Likewise, perfectly honest misidentifications can be hard to weed out, as exemplified by the photographs taken by the mountaineer Eric Shipton (1907–77) in the Himalayas in 1951. Here the confusion arises from the fact that two quite distinct sets of photographs were for a long time considered together. The first shows what looks like a trail left in the snow by a large, running biped. Not until the mid-1970s was it shown that this trail was almost certainly left by a mountain goat; it was then widely assumed that the other piece of photographic evidence could be similarly dismissed. But this – the famous five-toed footprint in the snow – certainly cannot be attributed to a mountain goat.

Exactly what it was remains something of an enigma. Footprints do funny things in snow because of melting and refreezing. When snow melts and then refreezes, a print that had been distorted by melting can be frozen in place, so that its origin is no longer at all evident. Thus Shipton's print might have started off as that of a human (a few hardy human ascetics roam the upper reaches of the Himalayas barefoot for religious reasons) or even as a composite made by a string of quadrupeds running in the footsteps of a group leader. Such speculations, of course, do not discount the possibility that it was made by a wild man.

Another famous piece of photographic evidence is the amateur film, purportedly of a Sasquatch, made in the autumn of 1967 by Roger Patterson. He was out riding with a friend in northern California when a female Sasquatch suddenly emerged from the trees ahead of them. Patterson's horse immediately threw him, but luckily he was still clutching his cine camera and had sufficient presence of mind to shoot 6–7m (20–23ft) of film as the creature rather lazily made its exit. This film has provided the basis for almost all media depictions of the Sasquatch.

**BELOW Roger Patterson and René Dahinden. Patterson (on right) holds a cast of a Bigfoot footprint found at Bluff Creek in 1964, three years before he shot his famous film. Dahinden, a veteran Bigfoot-hunter, is holding a cast of a footprint found after Patterson's disputed encounter with the creature.**

A frame from the most famous
Bigfoot film of them all, shot by Roger Patterson at Bluff Creek,
Northern California, on 20th October 1967, apparently showing a
female of the species. Many professional naturalists, basing their opinions
on disparities between the creature's proportions and its gait, etc., believe
that Patterson may have been the victim of a hoax. But the matter
remains unproven.

It has also, on occasion, been analysed by professional naturalists, and the verdict returned by these naturalists has been generally rather depressing for Bigfoot fans. Although the creature is quite apparently a female – it has clearly visible breasts – its gait is like that of a human male. It has pronounced human-like buttocks, unlike the apes (although this point does not contraindicate Bigfoot as an unknown hominid). Foot-size and stride-length do not match. This latter judgement obviously involves possibly false preconceptions as to the relationship between foot-size and stride-length; but the creature's gait can be seen to be more like that of a human being taking extended strides than that of a biped taking strides of a length to which it is accustomed.

The inevitable conclusion might seem to be that Patterson's film was a hoax; but Patterson was most manifestly convinced that what he filmed was what he saw, and the various researchers who have interviewed him seem unanimous as to his integrity. The next possible explanation – unless of course the naturalists, not all of whom are hostile to the notion that Bigfoot might exist, are just plain wrong in their interpretations of the film – is that *Patterson himself* was the victim of a hoax. This seems possible, since the top half of the filmed creature is, overall, bigger and bulkier than it ought to be in relation to the bottom half: a creature with such overall proportions would be a quadruped, rather than a biped. But a man in a gorilla costume? This could explain the bulky chest and broad shoulders compared with the less-padded legs. It has been widely suggested – without a shred of proof – that Patterson's companion on the riding expedition, Bob Gimlin, was "somewhat of a 'third man' character in this affair" (to quote one naturalist), and that he might have been responsible for setting up the encounter, originally with no more lofty intention than playing a rather elaborate joke on his gullible friend. However, it should be stressed that it is far from proven that there was any hoaxing involved: unknown animals, almost by definition, will break some of the general rules inferred by naturalists from their observations of known animals.

Even if Patterson's film might one day be shown to be the product of a trick, this would by no means show that other evidences of Bigfoot are fallacious. A very convincing piece of photographic evidence derives from an encounter in 1917 between an expedition led by a Swiss geologist, François de Loys, and a couple of large primates on the Venezuela/Colombia border. The primates were aggressive towards the expedition party, screaming shrilly and defecating into their own hands in order to create ammunition that could be hurled at the intruders – a typical aggressive response among the larger primates. The terrified humans shot at and killed the female; the male ran off.

## GEOGRAPHICAL DISTRIBUTION OF BIGFOOT

If we look at the geographical distribution of Bigfoot reports, we see what seems at first a further clue to the nature of the animal. Drawn on the world map, the area in which there have been sightings is vast but cohesive, running over much of Asia and then, via the Bering Strait (which until a few thousand years ago was closed, and served as a land-bridge across which various species are known to have migrated), into Canada and the states of Washington, Oregon and California, and thence into northern South America.

However, this observation in itself raises a problem: in Asia Bigfoot seems largely to be confined to remote fastnesses, but the same can no longer be said of all the North American venues, even the less populated of which are still teeming with human activity compared with the upper stretches of the Himalayas. While one can accept that mere chance might have dictated that we have yet to come across a Yeti fossil, it seems odd that we have no more tangible evidence of the Sasquatch than Patterson's (debated) fragment of movie, a number of reported encounters and a plethora of dubious footprints.

**LEFT** The corpse of a strangely manlike ape killed by François de Loys and his party on the Venezuela/ Colombia border in 1917.

The corpse was photographed, and we can deduce from that photograph that the primate was of the order of 1.5m (5ft) tall; de Loys himself measured it as 1.57m (5ft 1¾in). This certainly puts the creature firmly into the height-range of adult human beings, albeit a fairly short adult, but, just as importantly, means that the creature was far taller than any known New World primate. Moreover, the size of the forehead and the dentition seem to indicate that the creature is only remotely, if at all, related to the New World primates; and its overall appearance is definitely humanoid. It is possible that the beasts de Loys encountered were specimens of a species of highly advanced ape that has evolved independently in the Americas. This would seem to be borne out by the fact that the creature in the photograph has the flat female breasts typical of apes, not humans.

And not Yeti, either, if the legends from the Himalayas are to be believed: the Sherpas widely report that the females of the Yeti have breasts so huge and droopy that they have to throw them back over their shoulders, out of the way, in order to be able to run properly. It is probably safe to say that exaggeration has played a generous part in such tales, but the very fact that the exaggeration has been promulgated would seem to suggest that, like human women, Yeti females have protuberant rather than flat breasts. They are, therefore, in evolutionary terms a long way from the gorillas, chimps, orang-utans and other higher primates: they are much more like us. As we noted earlier, the assumption that all reported sightings of Bigfoot represent the same species is a convenience only: that good evidence exists of an unknown species of primate in South America should have no bearing on our evaluation of reports of wild men from other parts of the world.

# THE YETI

Let us return to the Yeti. As early as the 13th century, the English scholar Roger Bacon (*c*.1214–94) knew of stories about the wild men who inhabited the high mountains of the Far East. He described how the Asians would capture the beasts by leaving out dishes of fermented liquor; once the unfortunate creature had drunk itself into a stupor, the humans would move in. Their aim may have been to consume the animals' brains, for there is a long-standing belief that eating human brains can increase the eater's intelligence or, at the very least, provide a marijuana-like "high". Since there are taboos making it difficult to get hold of the real thing, subscribers to such beliefs over the centuries are known to have made do with second-best – i.e., ape brains. But of

LEFT A 17th-century engraving of a wild man reported from Java. Reports of wild men are frequent from all over the Orient.

course the Yeti, presumed to be closer than the apes to humanity, would supply an even closer approximation. But this is to digress.

In 1970, in Nepal, two mountaineers, Don Whillans and Dougal Haston (1940–77), came across a set of mysterious footprints at an altitude of about 4,000m (13,000ft). That night Whillans was looking out of his tent when he saw, some distance away in the moonlight, what seemed to him to be an ape-like creature, although he could

LEFT Dougal Haston, one of the mountaineers in Nepal who reportedly caught site of a Yeti.

see only that it was moving on all fours. Whillans told the Sherpas with the expedition that he had seen a Yeti, and later he led them past the trail of footprints that he and Haston had discovered. To his fascination the Sherpas completely ignored them. His impression was that they regarded the Yeti as a creature that, if left strictly alone, would return the compliment. In other words, far from being terrified of the creature – as sensationalist accounts would have us believe – the Sherpas display prudent caution and respect towards it.

This puts the Yeti into a rather different category from most other folk monsters, which are credited with rather nasty habits. The same is even more true of the Almas (discussed later in more detail), which are viewed by the peoples of Central Asia as a lesser form of human being but in no way as a malevolent one – indeed, if we are to believe the various accounts, people in those parts treat any Almas they might come across rather as you might treat a friendly dog you encountered in the street. Such an attitude would seem to suggest that the people who report meeting Almas are in fact telling the truth rather than stewing up a good yarn for the benefit of the tourists.

The earliest Western encounter with the Yeti appears to have been in 1889. Major L. A. Waddell, according to his book *Among the Himalayas*, was travelling in northeastern Sikkim when he came across a series of large footprints in the snow. The Sherpas with him claimed that these were the spoor of giant hairy wild men. Waddell's report perhaps created a greater sensation in the West than he had intended; certainly interest was intense by 1921 when a British expedition led by Colonel C. K. Howard Bury (1883–1963) was making an assault on Everest's North Face. During the ascent the party saw distant moving dots on the snow above them; when they reached the place where those dots had been, some 7,000m (23,000ft) up, the climbers found huge footprints. The Europeans, aware of the melting/refreezing effects already noted, concluded that the barely seen creatures must have been mountain wolves, but the Sherpas were confident in attributing them to the Yeti. (The term they used, *metoh kangmi*, translates as "abominable snowman" and, as such, became fashionable.) The expedition's account inspired other travellers to recall their own experiences. Here is William Knight (1858–1943), interviewed by *The Times* for 2 November 1921 issue about an encounter he had had in the region:

> I stopped to breathe my horse on an open clearing . . . . I heard a slight sound, and looking round, I saw some 15 or 20 paces away, a figure which I now suppose must have been one of the hairy men that the Everest Expedition talk about . . . . Speaking to the best of my recollection, he was a little under 1.83m (6ft) high, almost stark naked in that bitter cold – it was the month of November. He was a kind of pale yellow all over, about the colour of a Chinaman, a shock of matted hair on his head, little hair on his face, highly splayed feet, and large, formidable hands. His muscular development in the arms, thighs, legs and chest was terrific. He had in his hand what seemed to be some form of primitive bow.

The individual described by Knight does not seem to have been much like the hirsute monster of the sensationalist media; nor does he much resemble the version described by the Sherpas. A plausible explanation is that this was one of the mountain-roaming human ascetics mentioned above, and the same explanation was given by the Greek photographer and Fellow of the Royal Geographical Society N. A. Tombazi for an encounter which he recorded in 1925 in his *Account of a Photographic Expedition to the Southern Glaciers of Kangchenjunga in the Sikkim Himalaya*: "I

Alleged footprints of a Yeti; they
are quite similar in appearance to those of a man, but only 10cm (6 to
7in) at the broadest part of the foot.

conjecture then that this 'wild man' may be either a solitary or else a member of an isolated community of pious Buddhist ascetics, who have renounced the world and sought their God in the utter desolation of some high place, as yet undesecrated by the world." In 1964 Tombazi rejected this cautious (and rather poetic) conclusion: "I still carry a vivid impression of the glimpse I caught at the time, and am convinced that the Yeti in the form of a biped and not a quadruped is in existence."

Which of his two impressions of the experience is more likely to have been the correct one? Tombazi saw the creature at a distance of 200–300m (650–1,000ft). His description of the footprints he discovered on examining the place where he had seen it is of interest:

> They were similar in shape to those of a man, but only six to seven inches (15–18cm) long by four inches (10cm) wide at the broadest part of the foot. The marks of five distinct toes and the instep were perfectly clear, but the trace of the heel was indistinct, and the little that could be seen of it appeared to narrow down to a point . . .

His conclusion that he had seen a wandering ascetic would seem to be invalidated by these measurements, unless the ascetic was extremely small. Even if that were the case, the breadth of the feet in comparison with their length would seem to be far greater than that of any normal human foot. What, then, of Tombazi's description of the creature itself?

> Unquestionably, the figure in outline was exactly like a human being, walking upright and stopping occasionally to uproot or pull at some dwarf rhododendron bushes. It showed up dark against the snow and, as far as I could make out, wore no clothes.

### HUMAN·LIKE APPEARANCE

This insistence by Tombazi on the human-like appearance of the creature would seem to discount one of the other popular explanations of the Yeti, which ascribes all the footprints so far recorded to bears. Certainly, some of them have been shown to be bear prints – in certain circumstances ursine footprints can look remarkably like human ones, except they are much broader – but bears cannot be evoked to explain all such spoors. Neither can the Himalayan langur, which reaches a height of at most about 1.37m (4ft 6in), or the rather larger and more heavily built snow monkey (Roxellana's snub-nosed langur), which has a

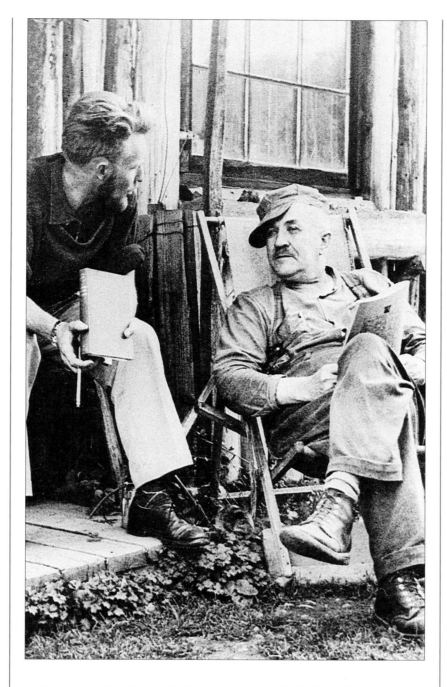

LEFT **Albert Ostman (right) being interviewed by John Green. In 1957 Ostman claimed that in 1924 he had been abducted by a family of Sasquatch in British Columbia.**

rather humanlike face and is known to attain high altitudes on occasion but which is rarely found in the southwestern Himalayas, the region from which most Yeti reports originate. Moreover, langurs have long, graceful toes, not short stubby ones like the footprints in the photographs taken by Shipton and others. Within the bounds of orthodox zoology, there seems to be no immediate explanation for these tracks.

# THE SASQUATCH

When settlers first arrived in what is now western North America the indigenous Amerindians recounted various tales of the wild man – the Sasquatch – who dwelt in desolate regions. Interestingly, these creatures were generally said to be notable because of the profusion of hair on their heads alone. With typical Western chauvinism, the newcomers dismissed such tales as primitive nonsense – although not such nonsense that the Sasquatch couldn't be blamed for a vicious double murder and mutilation in 1910 in Nahanni Valley (thereafter named Headless Valley), Northwest Territories, Canada. It was not until 1957, when an ex-lumberjack named Albert Ostman claimed to have been kidnapped in 1924 and held for several days by a family of Sasquatch – possibly for breeding purposes, since there was a spinster daughter Sasquatch – near Vancouver Island, that more credence began to be given to these tales. Ostman had kept silent about his experience for so long, he said, for fear of being treated as a crank. There are serious doubts about his account – notably that the Sasquatch's dietary regime he described would not have been adequate to keep the creatures alive – but, intriguingly, research at the time revealed that 1924 had been marked by another Sasquatch encounter: a coal miner called Fred Beck and his companions claimed to have had a running battle with a troop of the creatures in Ape Canyon, Washington State, after Beck had shot and killed one of them. Much later, in 1982, a logger, Rant Mullens, claimed that the story was born from a joke he and a friend had played on Beck and his companions: they had rolled rocks down onto the roof of the cabin in which the miners had sheltered, and terrified imaginations – as well as the human need for self-justification when fleeing from menace – had done the rest. However, the delay between the event and the "confession" (time enough for nearby Mount Helens to bury any evidence in a layer of ash) must cast doubt on Mullens' story.

Then we have the hairy biped captured in 1884 between Yale and Lytton near the Fraser River, British Columbia, and christened Jacko. Nothing remains of this creature, which fact has tempted many writers to dismiss it as a complete hoax dreamt up by newspapers. An alternative and rather attractive possibility is that it was a chimpanzee or other primate brought to North America as a pet – or, more likely, as a curio for display – and turfed out by its owner when it turned nasty. Barnum & Bailey's Circus later displayed what they claimed was the original Jacko; hmmm. Then there is Mo-Mo, the Missouri monster, which caused a sensation after being first encountered by a pair of young women near Louisiana, Missouri, in 1971. Their story had many of the

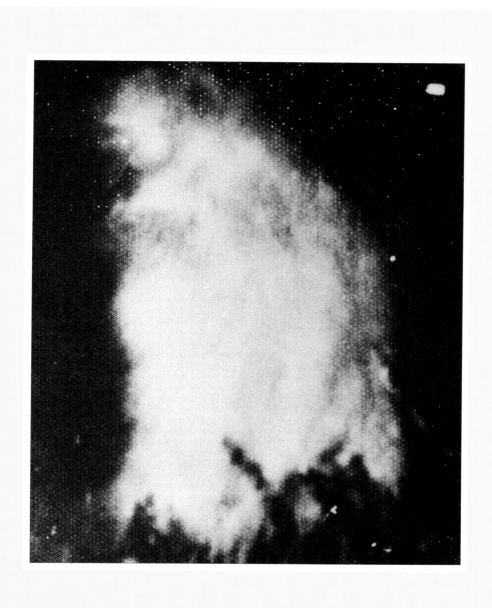

A lucky snap of a white Bigfoot
seen around Fort Worth, Texas, in 1969. The Lake Worth Monster, as
it came to be known, caused a considerable flap between July and
November of that year.

## THE ORANG PENDEK

*Langurs seem to have been responsible for the Sumatran version of the wild-man, the Orang Pendek. Standing anywhere between 75cm (30in) and 1.5m (5ft), these have head hair and a long mane of black, the rest of the body being covered in shortish black or brown hair. They are supposed to have their own language; some tales accord them the standard folkloric characteristic of having their feet on backwards. Examples of mummified Orang Pendeks were offered for sale by the Sumatrans to tourists even as early as the time of Marco Polo (c.1254–c.1324), who was lucky enough to see them being made from the corpses of langurs and other monkeys of suitable size.*

elements of phantom hitch-hiker legends: they stopped for a picnic, the big hairy monster appeared, they fled to the car leaving their keys in the open, the monster ate some of their picnic before ambling off about its own business. A determined search of the area the following year revealed nothing, not even a footprint (this very lack is a trifle surprising – you would have thought that hoaxers or sheer human credulity would have produced *something*); although records were discovered, dating back as far as the 1940s, of a gorilla-like creature having been observed in the Missouri marshlands. The Lake Worth Monster, first sighted in 1969 in Texas, caused a similar flap, during which there was a plenitude of reports of mutilations of domestic animals. The only properly verified casualty of the monster's bloodthirsty spree seems to have been an unfortunate teenager, wounded when shot by a fellow monster-hunter.

It was in 1958 that a truck driver called Jerry Crew discovered massive footprints in the mud surrounding his work-camp in Humboldt County, northern California. He followed the trail for a while without success, but quick-wittedly took a plaster-cast of one of the footprints; photographs of him holding the cast appeared nationwide, caused a sensation and ensured that the name Bigfoot, rather than Sasquatch, became firmly enshrined in the North American popular consciousness. In 1969, near Bossburgh, Washington State, a continuous trail of 1089 footprints, running for about a kilometre (1,000 yards), was found: at one point the creature making them, evidently crippled in the right leg, had casually stepped over a 1.1m (43in) fence, so the legs must have been long – and the feet large: the prints were 45cm (17½in) by 18cm (7in). And in 1974 a lumberjack called Jack Cochran, working in the Hood River National Forest, Oregon, saw a huge hairy humanoid standing some 50m (46 yards) from him; he had just disabused himself of the hypothesis that this was one of his logging colleagues playing around when the beast wandered off. A day or so later a couple of his companions, Fermin Osborne and a young man called Tom, encountered the creature and gave chase, without either subtlety or success. Investigators who came to the site later – led by Peter Byrne of the Bigfoot Information Center, The Dalles – found huge footprints intermingled with those of the pursuing loggers.

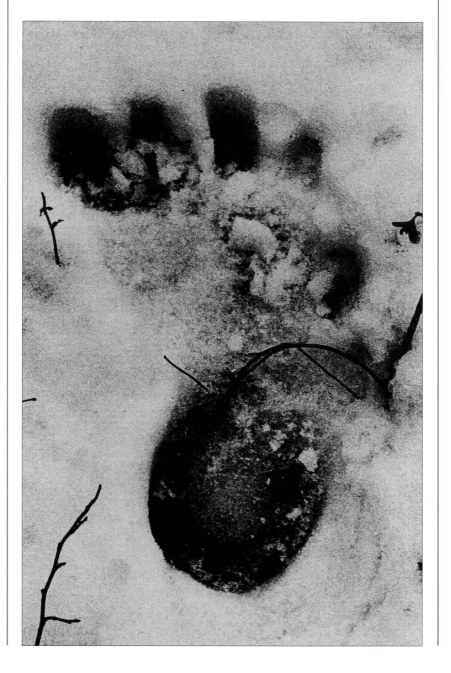

LEFT One of over a thousand Bigfoot footprints found in snow at Bossburg, Washington State, in 1969. The print is 42cm (16½in) long and seems to be deformed.

# THE MINNESOTA ICEMAN

In the 1960s Frank K. Hansen showed around Midwest carnivals a block of ice containing what was claimed to be a Bigfoot-style creature or, possibly, either a survival or a well-preserved fossil of one of our hominid ancestors. It was Hansen's claim that the hairy body had been discovered in a vast block of ice in the Bering Strait. In late 1968 news of the exhibit reached distinguished cryptozoologist Ivan T. Sanderson (1911–73), who tracked it down to a small farm near Winona, Mississippi, where Hansen stored it during the off-season. Bernard Heuvelmans was in the USA at the time, and Sanderson asked him if he would like to come along and help to examine the enigma. By this time it was realized that the body could not be a fossil: fossils do not normally have as cause of death a gun shot through the right eye. It seemed, therefore, that it must be – if anything – a variety of Bigfoot. Both Sanderson and Heuvelmans were sufficiently impressed to bring out separate scientific papers proclaiming that the creature was indeed a genuine hominid. Then Hansen's story began to change.

First it was announced that Hansen was not the Iceman's owner, merely its manager; the real owner was a Hollywood millionaire who wished to remain anonymous. This mystery man had picked up the corpse in Hong Kong, from where it had travelled by a circuitous route to reach the USA. The millionaire was not interested in his "fossil" being subjected to scientific examination; instead, he was determined that it be on show so that the "common man" could make up his own mind. Hansen, his obedient servant, returned the Iceman to the carnival circuit; but this time there were problems, because quite clearly the exhibit had altered; whereas before it had had but a single tooth, it was now the proud owner of four. Hansen admitted that he had substituted a latex model for the original.

Then a woman called Helen Westring hit the headlines with her claim that, a few years earlier, she had been alone in Minnesota woodlands when a great pink-eyed monster with huge hairy hands had raped her. Afterwards she had been able to grab her rifle and put a bullet through the rapist's eye. Here, then, was another explanation of the beast's origin. Hansen seemed briefly to accept the claim – he depicted himself as the lucky discoverer of the corpse that Westring had left behind her – but then he decided that he preferred the limelight for himself. The "true" story was that, seven or eight years earlier, while in the USAF, he had been hunting with companions when he had startled and then shot the wild man. He had left the corpse in the snow for a couple of months before returning to reclaim it for storage in a deep-freeze. Later he had moved the body to his Winona farm, preparatory to taking it out on tour – which it, or its latex replica, still was as late as the 1980s. It is this plethora of diverse claims that caused Sanderson and Heuvelmans to give up the whole affair as the fraud that it almost certainly was – the words "almost certainly" being added for scientific rectitude rather than for any reasons of doubt.

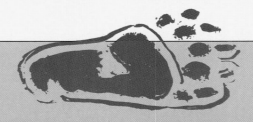

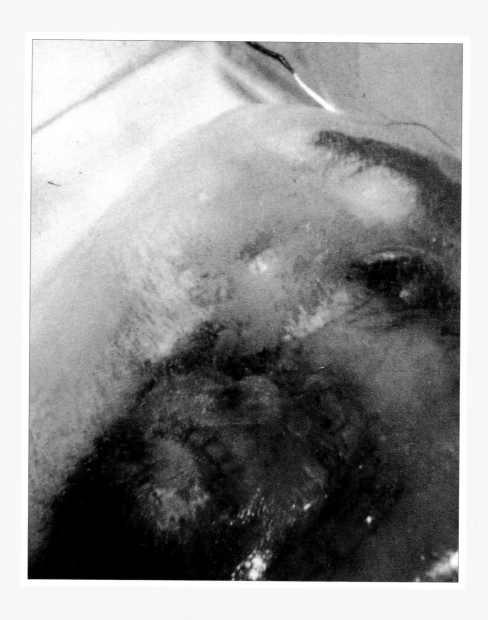

Arare photograph of the
Minnesota Iceman; the bigfoot-type creature that proved to be a fake.

## OTHER SIGHTINGS

An Illinois war veteran reported twice seeing a Sasquatch with a chilling difference: the creature had three legs. From Ohio come reports of Orange Eyes, a Bigfoot standing up to 3.4m (11ft 2in) tall, covered in orange fur and with eyes that glow in the dark: since the beast makes a habit of haunting lovers' lanes, thereby disrupting adolescent in-car entertainment, it is not surprising that concrete evidence is not forth-coming. There are similar reports from elsewhere in the USA – Arkansas, for example, has the celebrated Fouke Monster – although the variant reported from Prince George's County, Virginia, is of some psychological interest: dubbed the Goatman, this beast has a human top half and a goatish lower half, thereby resembling a Greek satyr.

Of all these regional humanoid monsters, only Florida's Skunk Ape seems to have been clumsy enough to permit more coherent sightings of itself. Although stories about this beast have been in circulation since

**RIGHT Paul Freeman holding a plastercast of a footprint of the creature he claims to have seen on 10th June 1982 in Umatilla National Forest, near Walla Walla, Washington State.**

at least the early decades of this century, it was only in the late 1960s and early 1970s that it became a national celebrity. As one might guess from its name, it is said to smell worse than a barrel of skunks – an attribute it shares with Mo-Mo and the Yeti. A man named *Ralph Chambers* reported sighting it in 1966; he tried to track it with his dogs, but the stench was so powerful that they refused. However, when the animal turned up in his back yard in the following year they attacked it; it seemed unconcerned and ambled off. In 1970 a party of amateur archaeologists were at work on an Amerindian burial mound when they saw the Skunk Ape. They measured the footprints it left as 45cm (17½in) long and 29cm (11½in) across at the toes. In 1973 the driver of an automobile claimed to have hit one of the creatures as it stepped out into the road in front of him; it limped away. Analyses of the blood and fur it left on his car proved inconclusive. All of the descriptions given suggested that the creatures were Sasquatch rather than typical lovers'-lane monsters; but by this period, of course, the image of the Sasquatch was well known to the American public, and so it is perfectly possible that the witnesses, quite unconsciously, tailored their memories of what they had seen to fit the "accepted stereotype".

Many of the Sasquatch tales evaporate on closer examination, and must be regarded as inevitable by-products of a media-dependent culture. Some are known hoaxes, like the notorious Minnesota Iceman (see page 24). Other evidences are more interesting – John Napier, one of the very few academics seriously to have studied Bigfoot, regards the Bossburgh trail as being by far the most convincing – but all of them display the same unsatisfying characteristic of unprovability. This is astonishing. As noted, the Sasquatch frequents areas that are often far from remote; moreover, determined Sasquatch-hunts have been periodically mounted – not always by callow, trigger-happy teenagers but sometimes by dedicated and at least quasi-scientific researchers – yet nothing more tangible than plaster-casts has yet been discovered. It would require a very intelligent, very well organized or perhaps just very fortunate monster indeed to have completely evaded all of those hunters. If we bear in mind that man-hunts, seeking murderers and the like, are generally successful, even though it is easier for human beings than for looming hairy monsters to lose themselves in the throng, the Sasquatch's complete escape seems incredible. Indeed, one would be tempted to dismiss the whole modern Sasquatch industry – for industry it is in many parts of North America – as nothing more than a monumental hoax or a communal delusion were it not for the sheer volume of reports. John Napier has remarked that it is hard to credit that there could be so many liars or victims of self-delusion.

ABOVE **Dr John Napier, the naturalist whose study of the worldwide Bigfoot phenomenon, *Bigfoot: The Yeti and Sasquatch in Myth and Reality* (1972), remains probably the most impressive piece of research on the topic and brought much-needed respectability to the field.**

# THE ALMA

Returning to Asia, this time to the northeast, we discover the Almas, which are noteworthy among all the Bigfoot clans in that they are generally reported as being more closely human than are the Yeti and Sasquatch. The classic encounter took place in 1957, when a Leningrad University hydrologist, Dr Alexander G. Pronin, was a member of an expedition at work in the Baliand-Kiik River valley in the Pamir Mountains. According to a newspaper interview published a few months later, it was "a manlike creature walking on two feet, slightly stooping, and wearing no clothes. Its thickest body was covered in reddish-grey hair, and it had long arms." Pronin was lucky enough to see the creature – or another like it – a few days later. He suspected it of "borrowing" one of the expedition's boats for a bit of joy-riding. When Pronin's account was published it was derided by most Soviet scientists – most, but not all. Researchers such as Professor Jeanne Kofman have collected scores of Alma legends from the herdsmen of the area, and the fact that the descriptions have been similar to Pronin's has been taken as strong evidence that more than a myth is stalking the wildernesses of northeast Asia. A certain Professor Stanyukovic led a nine-month expedition of archaeologists, botanists, hunters and zoologists into the Pamirs in 1959 with the specific purpose of tracking down the Alma. Snares were set, living bait staked out and telescopic-lensed cameras poised, but neither hide, hair nor footprint was detected; what the expedition did find was a considerable deal of evidence, in the form of cave paintings, artefacts and so on, that the region had been well populated by mankind in the Neolithic Age. Another scientist to take the Alma seriously was Dr Boris F. Porshnev, a historian of science, who became head of the Soviet Academy of Science's grandiosely named Commission for Studying the Question of the Abominable Snowman. Much earlier, in 1881, Colonel Nikolai Mikhailovic Przewalski (1839–88), had collected tales of wild men in Mongolia. V. A. Khaklov, a zoologist, collected many accounts in the early part of this century; one of these is of special interest in that it describes the behaviour of a (female) Alma:

> The creature was usually quite silent and bared her teeth on being approached. She had a peculiar way of lying down; she squatted on her knees and elbows, resting her forehead on the ground, and her hands were folded over the back of her head. She would eat only raw meat, some vegetables and gravy, and sometimes insects that she caught. When drinking water would lap, or sometimes dip her arm into the water and then lick her fur.

BELOW "Bigfoot naturalists" René Dahinden and Dr Jeanne Kofman with their Soviet counterparts, Dmitri Bayanov and Lt-Col V. S. Karapetian (left), in Russia in 1972.

BOTTOM The science historian Dr Boris F. Porshnev photographed in 1972, when he was head of the Soviet Academy of Science's Commission for Studying the Question of the Abominable Snowman. The plastercast is of a wild-man footprint.

ABOVE **Drawing of a wild man seen by Lt-Col V. S. Karapetian in 1941 near Buinakask, Dagestan (then part of the Soviet Union).**

This was, of course, a captive Alma, so we should not perhaps read too much significance into the minutiae of her behaviour. However, we can note the relative pacificivity, the intelligence and the dietary regime: it was their reported vegetarian habits, we recall, that threw most doubt on the existence of the Sasquatch family that kidnapped Albert Ostman. And it is behaviour that most distinguishes the Almas from other creatures like the Yeti. There are accounts of Almas warming themselves at unattended campfires (most wild animals distrust fire) or even breast-feeding human children. And there are even rumours of half-caste offspring between humans and Almas; whether or not these rumours are true is debatable, but the fact that they can be believed indicates that the peoples of these remote regions regard the Almas as human beings, albeit of a rather lowly sort.

Outside the main regions we have been discussing – Asia, North America and northern South America – there are fewer folkloric tales of wild men and barely any that have survived into the modern age. Early European explorers in Africa were startled by some of the stories that they were told, but soon found that indeed there *were* people of very tall and very small stature. The Ainu of Japan, differentiated from the mainstream population by their pale skins, stockiness, Australoid features and hirsuteness (and now very largely absorbed into the main stock), have a problematic racial history and a language (now almost extinct) that bears no relation to any other human tongue. The "wild men" of Tasmania, hunted as game by the "civilized" white incursors during the 19th century, proved to be a mild-mannered people of the same basic stock as the Maoris; this was discovered after the predations of the "sportsmen" had reduced them to a few individuals, the last of whom died a few years later. There are still "wild men" in the South American rain forests, despite the efforts of various governments to exterminate them; but these peoples are, like the Ainu and the Tasmanians, very similar to the main stock of humankind.

In medieval Europe there were many tales of wild men but few attempts to explain them. It is thus hard to establish whether the traditions were referring to human beings who had said farewell to society and gone off to inhabit the wild places or, instead, to beings – or remembered beings – who came of different stock from the rest of humanity. A persistent tradition was that wild women had such droopy breasts that they had to throw the appendages over their shoulders in order to run properly; this characteristic has been noted in connection with the Yeti, but we should beware of reading too much into what may be only an example of cross-cultural fertilization, with European myths fuelling Asian ones or vice versa. The figure of Caliban in Shakespeare's *The Tempest* (*c*.1611) may represent a late hangover from the European wild man tradition or may be derived from tales brought to England by travellers from afar.

Certainly it is tempting to think that the European tales might reflect the existence in that continent until at least the Dark Ages of relations of the Asian and North American Bigfoot. If such creatures were to be exterminated anywhere, deliberately or inadvertently, by the spread of *Homo sapiens* it would be in crowded Europe. That there is considerable overlap between these wild man tales and those concerning werewolves and vampires is, if anything, a support to such notions; for these creatures were likewise regarded as being in some fashion a bastardized version of humanity.

**RIGHT One of the Chinese scientists who have taken reports of wild men very seriously indeed: Dr Zhou Guoxing searching for evidence in Shennongjia Forestry Region, Hubei Province, China, in 1977.**

**CENTRE A Chinese poster depicts a hairy hominid. Its caption reads in part: "Have You Seen the Wild Man?"**

### FINDINGS

What, then, can we conclude about the nature of Bigfoot, worldwide? John Napier and Bernard Heuvelmans (b.1916) are without doubt the two most distinguished naturalists, outside the Soviet Union, to have studied the evidence, printed or otherwise, concerning Bigfoot. Napier, although troubled by the Shipton photographs, concludes that the Yeti is a myth. He concedes the exciting possibility that the Almas might be descendants of Neanderthal Man (we recall that Professor Stanyukovic's

expedition discovered widespread Neolithic cultural remains), but considers it more likely that they are "human beings, perhaps the remnants of a primitive, culturally archaic population that has survived in the empty mountain regions of Central Asia for many thousands of years". He is "convinced that the Sasquatch exists" but comes close to admitting that his reasons are more visceral than anything else.

Heuvelmans was considerably more receptive to the idea that the Yeti exists, considering the Alma to be merely another form of Yeti; he was less knowledgeable about the Sasquatch. He reckoned that, if it is a relic of one of the hominid primates that form a truncated branch of our evolutionary tree, then the most likely candidate is probably *Gigantopithecus*; he suggested that, until we have a specimen to examine in order to check this possibility, we should at least give the Yeti a proper taxonomic name, *Dinanthropoides nivalis*, meaning "terrible anthropoid of the snows". His brief zoological summary of the creature is worth quoting *in extenso*:

> We have reason to believe that it is a large biped anthropoid ape, from 5 to 8 feet (1.52–2.44m) high according to its age, sex, or geographic race, which lives in the rocky area at the limit of the plant line on the slopes of the whole Himalayan range. It has plantigrade feet (i.e., the entire sole touches the ground in walking), and the very conspicuous big toe, unlike that of most monkeys, is not opposable to the other toes. It walks with its body leaning slightly forward; its arms are fairly long and reach down to its knees. It has a flat face, a high forehead, and the top of its skull is shaped like the nose of an artillery shell; its prognathism (protrusion of jaw) is slight, but its thick jaws have developed considerably in height, hence the disproportionate size of its molars. To this outsize masticatory apparatus are connected very powerful jaw muscles. On the cranium there is a sagittal (i.e., running from front to back of skull) crest which is revealed by a thickening of the scalp in the adult male, at least, and the presence of upstanding hair. It is covered with thick fur . . . It appears to be omnivorous: roots, bamboo shoots, fruit, insects, lizards, birds, small rodents, and occasionally larger prey like yaks are all grist to its mill in such barren country.

The final sentence of Heuvelmans' zoological summary is perhaps the most interesting – and perhaps the most disturbing – of all: "Its cerebral capacity should be about equal to or even greater than man's."

# CHAPTER TWO

# WILD
# ANIMALS

One of the more curious cases in the files of the unexplained concerns an incident that occurred in 1855 in the county of Devon near the southwest tip of the UK. On the night of 7 February of that year a carpet of snow lay across the land. The next morning, people over a large area of the county were surprised to discover, still clearly marked in the snow, footprints of an apparently bipedal creature, which, it seemed, had wandered not only along thoroughfares but also through gardens and yards, over the roofs of some houses, right through a wall 4m (13ft) high, and even, near the estuary of the River Exe, across a 3km (2mi) stretch of running water, continuing again on the far bank as if the river in between had not been there at all. Soon the marks, which could be tracked for a frequently disrupted distance of about 150km (94mi) or more, had been christened the Devil's Footprints. Each measured about 10cm long by 7cm wide (4 × 2¾in), and they looked a little like the hoofprints of a pony – yet the creature responsible was certainly not four-legged and, besides, what pony could walk through a wall or over a rooftop?

In terms of physical reality, the mystery of the Devil's Footprints will probably never be solved, although numerous attempts have been made to pin the blame on one wild animal or another. It is certainly true that in certain circumstances the tracks of a quadruped in snow can resemble those of a biped, but what biped would normally traverse about 150km (94mi) in the six-hour period between the last fall of snow and the first observation of the tracks? Hoaxers would have to be superhumanly enthusiastic (or feasibly religiously zealous) about their prank to go to such extremes, and anyway their activities would almost certainly have been detected during the night unless they maintained a strict silence – difficult to do while trying to coordinate matching tracks on both sides of a 3km (2mi) river! The evidence was destroyed, of course, by the melting of the snow, thus rendering the mystery even further from solution.

**ABOVE** Big-cat tracks found in snow in North Devon, UK, in 1985. The hunt for the Exmoor Beast, as it is called, continues.

One of the suggested possibilities was that the tracks might have been made by a pair of kangaroos that had recently escaped from a zoo or circus nearby, and although in this instance the suggestion was useless – the prints in no way resembled those a kangaroo could leave – it does point to a more general likelihood that we shall return to on occasion during this chapter: that many of the mysterious animals reported to haunt various regions of the world may simply be escapees from menageries, or more probably, the descendants of escapees that learnt to adapt to their unusual environment. A different possibility, which we shall not discuss in any great detail, is that the Devil's Footprints incident was only a less easily rationalized instance of wild animal manifestations, in that normal sightings of such creatures are in fact paranormal rather than physical events: to summarize this hypothesis – by saying that the great majority of mysterious wild animals are in fact "phantoms" confirmed by the observer would be unjustly to oversimplify, but that is the general proposal. (Readers who wish to pursue the matter in depth are recommended to read Jenny Randles's (b. 1951) *Mind Monsters*.) A more prosaic possibility was suggested to me some years ago by Geoffrey A. Household, editor of a book on the subject. Household summed up his view in a letter to Colin Wilson:

> I think that Devonport Dockyard released, by accident, some sort of experimental balloon. It broke free from its moorings, and trailed two shackles on the end of ropes. The impressions left in the snow by these shackles went up the sides of houses, over haystacks, etc. . . . A Major Carter, a local man, tells me that his grandfather worked at Devonport at the time, and that the whole thing was hushed up because the balloon destroyed a number of conservatories, greenhouses, windows, etc. He says that the balloon finally came down at Honiton.

# EUROPEAN WILDCATS

## THE EXMOOR BEAST

Devon today is not a county unused to reports of curious wild animals. At least since the early 1980s farmers on and around Exmoor have been reporting the activities of some large predator that takes its toll of their sheep and lambs. Its customary method of killing is to crush the skull or break the neck of its victim; it then rips open the cadaver and eats the soft parts. It seems to kill not for the sake of killing but purely for food

BELOW **Found in North Devon, UK, in 1986 and assumed to have been a victim of the Exmoor Beast, this mutilated sheep's carcase was still warm on discovery.**

RIGHT **A cast of the pawprint of a big cat seen by a West Devon (UK) farmer in 1964. The cast measures about 13cm (5in) across.**

or in battle with any other animal foolish enough to take it on. For example, John and Dorothy Youé of Dunkeswell, near Honiton, reported in 1991 that an aggressive cat of theirs died some while after having had a raucous scrap one night with an unknown antagonist; the vet performing the autopsy discovered that the fatal wound had been inflicted by what appeared to be the tooth of a lynx or similar large cat. And it is at this stage that confusion enters for, while lynx hair has indeed been discovered at the sites of some of the Exmoor Beast's killings, elsewhere puma hair has been found. Moreover, the descriptions of the creature given by eyewitnesses differ radically from each other: some would fit a lynx (except with a bushy tail), some a puma, some a panther and some just an exceptionally large tabby wildcat of the type indigenous to more northerly parts of the UK; leopards have been implicated, too. Yet spoor has also been discovered near some of the kills that would suggest an outsize dog! It is not likely that a motley colony of animals could all be coexisting in such a way, but that is what the evidence would appear to indicate. This diversity of species points us away from the likelihood that the Beast – or, more accurately, Beasts – can be explained in terms of unknown native creatures and towards the possibility that a collection of animals was at some time in the early 1980s released on to Exmoor. Since large cats are dangerous animals – even if habitually as shy of human beings as the Exmoor Beast seems to be – it is not surprising that anyone who, say, disposed of an inherited collection of exotic pets in this way would keep quiet about having done so.

A similar explanation may account for a curious beast that caused considerable mayhem – reportedly killing several human beings as well as livestock – in Orel Province, Russia, for several months during 1893. Here again there was confusion as to the nature of the creature, originally described as an escaped panther. Soon, however, it was being described as any of a number of species of large cats, and even as a wolf; there were some among the people trying to track and destroy it who declared that it was a large dog of some kind. The beast vanished, apparently after having been poisoned, and so the mystery has never been solved. However, it was then quite common for the aristocracy in that part of the world to keep panthers and large dogs together in private menageries – not to mention in ones dedicated to public exhibition – and so it seems very likely that the confusion of descriptions results from a pair having escaped together.

## THE SURREY PUMA

Returning to the south of England the most famous mystery animal aside from the Exmoor Beast is almost certainly the Surrey Puma, reports of which have been made since at least the 1940s and more probably the 1930s, and which continue until this day. This long period of record would imply that the beasts concerned cannot simply be escapees, as the Exmoor Beast creatures certainly can: there must be a viable breeding population of large cats in and around Surrey. Although there are periodic claims that the animal has been shot, these are rapidly forgotten as soon as yet another domestsicated animal has been slain. In 1984 sample hairs were positively identified as belonging to a puma, although this does not completely rule out the presence of some form of unknown indigenous large cat whose hair, nowhere matched in the zoological records, is enough like that of a puma for the obvious, but wrong, conclusion to be drawn.

Many other areas of England have their own mysterious large cats, some being apparently present for only a season or two, others seemingly being or having become permanent residents. Moving north to Scotland we find the same pattern continuing, although here there is quite conclusive evidence of the existence of cats that were until recently unrecognized in that a few examples of one of these "mystery" species have since the 1980s been killed and examined. The exact taxonomic status of this creature, the Kellas cat, has not yet been determined, but the breed seems to have been in existence for as long as recorded history, if we are to accept the countless references to black wildcats in Scottish folklore. A similar creature has been reported from Transcaucasia, and it seems likely that the two are closely related.

ABOVE **Photographed from a distance of about 35m in 1966 at Worplesdon, Surrey, UK, a creature which the photographers were certain was not a feral tomcat. This is one of the clearest pictures of what came to be known as the Surrey Puma.**

BELOW **One of the wild cats that didn't get away. This creature was shot at Kellas, Grampian Region, Scotland, in 1983. Its exact taxonomic status has yet to be determined.**

Ireland is unusual in having no recognized forms of wildcat at all – there haven't even been any fossil finds. It seems very strange that the common species of wildcat, *Felix sylvestris*, found on the mainland (almost exclusively in Scotland), has not found its way across the Irish Sea. Certainly, though, there have been persistent reports for a long time of some sort of wild, catlike creature existing in Ireland. Sometimes these have been dismissed as merely domestic cats that have gone feral, but this seems impossible because most reports have stressed that the animals concerned were much larger than a domestic cat (feral cats, naturally, are of the same size as the domestic stock from which they have come). There has also been a degree of confusion because in Ireland the pine marten is often called a cat (usually a tree cat, to distinguish it from any other). Nevertheless, it seems certain that Ireland is indeed the home of some sort of unrecognized native (or naturalized) wildcat, with the added feature of interest that all the descriptions seem to point to a creature that is more like its African counterparts than its mainland-British ones.

### NORTH AMERICAN WILD CATS

North America is home to a number of recognized species of wildcats, the most populous and widely spread being the puma (known also under diverse names including cougar, panther and mountain lion). There is considerable debate as to the modern range of these creatures: for example, although it has been assumed since a little before the start of this century that the once prolific Eastern cougar had been extinguished through the depredations of humankind, there are occasional reports of individuals having been shot or at least sighted. Quite possibly the infamous Beast of Truro, Cape Cod, was just such a one: for a period of several months it was held responsible for slaying numerous domesticated animals.

### THE BLACK PANTHER

A much more mysterious North American creature is the famous black panther. The word "panther" strictly means simply "leopard", although its use commonly implies a leopard that, rather than being spotted in the normal fashion, is more or less black from head to tail. Even in an area where spotted leopards are relatively common, the black panther should be a pretty rare sight; in North America, where there are no spotted leopards at all except perhaps a few zoo or circus escapees, black panthers should be completely nonexistent – or, to turn this around, should black panthers be seen, so should spotted ones. To call the beast a panther is, therefore, to use something of a misnomer: all we

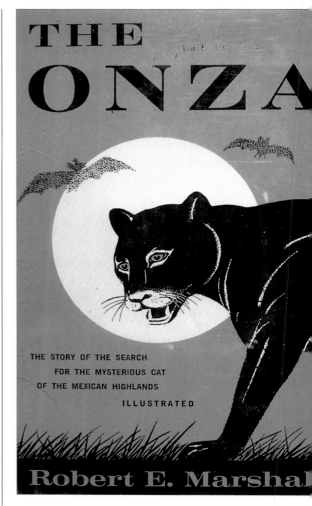

THE
ONZA

THE STORY OF THE SEARCH
FOR THE MYSTERIOUS CAT
OF THE MEXICAN HIGHLANDS
ILLUSTRATED

Robert E. Marshall

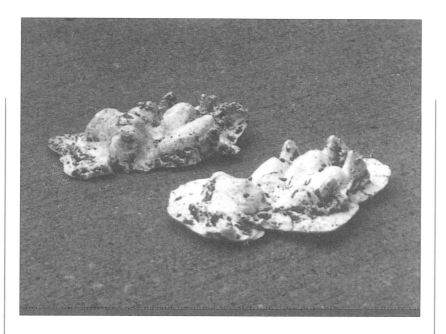

can say is that it is extremely like a panther in appearance.

There are a number of other possibilities that have been suggested. Among these are the jaguarundi, not generally known north of Central America but certainly dwelling in Texas as late as the end of last century, and with rare "wanderers" from the south still *very* occasionally venturing this far; the black jaguar, seemingly as unlikely a choice as the black leopard, but rendered more possible by the facts that jaguars were, until the beginning of this century, native to some parts of the USA (although rare) and that melanism (blackness) is much commoner among jaguars than among leopards; and the fisher, an animal of the marten family (as are, for example, otters and badgers) and therefore not a feline at all, but which is often black, has rather cat-like face and ears, can look a lot larger than it is because of its bushiness, can move with a cat-like grace and has a range extending through the northeastern USA and much of Canada.

One curious fact about black panthers is that, on those occasions when they are shot, they seem almost always to be able to drag themselves far enough away that the body is never recovered. On the rare instances when this has not happened, the carcase has somehow been lost before it can be subjected to proper zoological analysis. This lack of available specimens does lead one reluctantly towards the sort of parapsychological hypotheses noted above; it could also lead one to suspect hoaxing, but it is hard to imagine it on such a grand scale.

Other mysterious North American cats include the wampuses of central Missouri (amphibious) and Arkansas (whistling). Then there are the sap-drinking cactus cats of Arizona, the vast wowzer of Oklahoma (like a puma but several times the size) and the santer of North Carolina (probably some escaped exotic cat, although a few accounts describe it as doglike).

# WILD LIONS

Rarer and equally inexplicable are the reports from North America of wild lions, complete with manes and not at all like the mountain lion (i.e., puma). In 1877 near Sun, Indiana, Mary Crane and her boyfriend were walking in the woods when they were attacked by what may have been either a lion or a panther. The lad fled as Crane fainted, and when she awoke she found herself flat on her back with the beast licking her face; fortunately the animal was distracted by the sound of approaching rescuers and fled. The most famous early report came in 1917 from near the Sangamon River in Illinois. The beast concerned, nicknamed Nellie, was generally described as a lioness, and during the hunt mounted for her there were occasional sightings of a somewhat larger animal with a full mane, which was for obvious reasons assumed to be her mate. Neither cat was caught, and so our first assumption must be that they were zoo escapees. In 1948 one or two leonine creatures were seen in the vicinity of Abington, Indiana, by a number of witnesses over a period of a few days. There were a couple of sightings near Roscoe, Illinois, in 1970. Nearly a year later, again in Illinois but this time near Centralia, what seemed to the witness like a smallish lion was seen, although its face seems to have been hideous rather than leonine. In 1977 in Muscatine, Iowa, the police discovered a two-month-old lion cub; they advertised for any circus or menagerie that might have mislaid one, but there was no respone (even so, this surely must have been an escapee!). Karl P. N. Shuker, from whose Mystery Cats of the World most of that sample was drawn, suggests that there are three possible candidates for the creatures that have been described as lions. The idea that they might be large dogs he dismisses on the reasonable grounds that none of them has been reported to have barked. That they are escapees is, he claims, incontrovertible in most if not all cases: he points the finger not only at zoos and circuses but also at the revolting pastime that some rich Texans have discovered: importing at colossal expense rare African lions, releasing them into a wild area and then having a home-grown big-game shoot. His third proposal is, as he concedes, considerably less likely but nevertheless fun to think about. During the time of the Bering landbridge Old World lions were able to cross into the New World, where they developed as a distinct subspecies known as the American lion, or Panthera leo atrox (regarded by some palaeontologists as, in fact, a fully separate species, Panthera atrox). This creature is thought to have died out 10,000 years or so ago, but some researchers have suggested that small populations may have survived until the present. As Shuker points out, the theory collapses for a number of different reasons, including the fact that there are no recorded sightings of prides of North American lions.

# WILD KANGAROOS

Before we leave North America, it's worth glancing briefly at some reports of wild kangaroo-like creatures. Reports of North American kangaroos are not frequent, but they are sufficiently strange that one is reluctant to dismiss them. In most cases all the possible kangaroo-owners in the region concerned have been contacted to ensure that the animal is not an escapee; while it is possible that people would not admit to having mislaid a dangerous large cat, it is much less likely that they would try to cover up the loss of a kangaroo. It should be stressed, also, that the kangaroo rat of North America, a desert animal, although it hops along in kangaroo-like fashion, is tiny in comparison with the creatures reported and is distinguished by its exceptionally long tail.

Perhaps the best documented of the kangaroo cases is the one centred on Chicago, Illinois, in 1974. On 18 October 1984 the police received a call from a man who said there was a kangaroo outside his house; he and the police made the obvious assumption that it was an escapee. The patrolmen chased the animal into a cul-de-sac, where it drove them back with powerful kicks; while they decided whether or not they should shoot it, it hopped over a fence and made its escape. Exactly as one would expect, whatever the beast's origins, there were many scattered reports of sightings in that part of Chicago over the next few days: as would any escaped zoo animal, the kangaroo was wandering around, rootling through dustbins for food. Then, however, it headed out of the big city, being spotted in a number of towns to the west; about 10 days later it was seen in Indiana. A little over a month after its first appearance the kangaroo had vanished, presumably having simply

ABOVE **Casts of the footprints of a mystery kangaroo found at Brookfield Township, Wisconsin, in April 1978.**

LEFT **A polaroid photograph of a mystery kangaroo observed at Waukesha, Wisconsin, on 24th April 1978. This was a rather late appearance: most of the spate of kangaroo sightings in the Midwest occurred during 1974–6.**

Engraving by Gustave Doré.
Legends of colossal predatory birds carrying off humans are nothing new:
giant kites seem to have done little else, if we are to believe *The 1001
Nights' Entertainment.*

starved to death. The only problem with such a mundane explanation is that the kangaroo reappeared in the same general region in 1975 and 1976. The whole matter remains something of a puzzle, as does the earlier Big Bunny affair around Coon Rapids, Minnesota. Here the animal gained its nickname because almost all of those who saw it over a period of years were small children.

# THUNDERBIRDS

North America would seem also to be the home of some superlarge predatory birds. Instances of large eagles carrying away small children are rare but not unrecorded. A beast that in 1895 in Webster County, West Virginia, carried off in succession a 10-year-old girl, a hunting dog, a fawn and (almost certainly) a sheep was described by one witness as having a wingspan of about 4.5–5.5m (15–18ft). Much more recently, in July 1977, one of a pair of somewhat smaller (2.5m/8ft wingspan) but extremely powerful birds succeeded in grabbing 10-year-old Marlon Lowe in the family garden in Lawndale, Illinois; he survived the experience because his mother ran to help him, but by the time the bird released him it had raised him at least a couple of metres (6ft 6in) above the ground. A number of suggestions have been made that these birds could have been giant condors, wandering far from home, but this hypothesis fails for the cogent reason that condors feed on carrion, not living animals. Certainly there would seem to be a plausible connection between these recent reports and the Amerindian legends of vast creatures called thunderbirds.

Some more adventurous cryptozoologists have linked thunderbirds to surviving giant pterosaurs; they cite as support the fact that fossils of such creatures, with wingspans of the order of 15m (50ft), have been discovered in North America.

LEFT **Marlon and Ruth Lowe standing on the line of flight taken by the pair of big birds that came to their garden in Lawndale, Illinois, in 1977. One of the birds snatched Marlon from the ground; fortunately his mother ran to his assistance.**

# ANTIPODEAN MONSTERS

## THE TASMANIAN TIGER

In Australia, although there are equivalents of North America's black panther and UK beasts such as the Surrey Puma, much of the discussion of wild monsters centres on the Tasmanian tiger (or thylacine) and the Queensland tiger. The zoological standing of the former is not in any doubt; what is at question is whether or not any individuals of the species still survive. This large carnivorous marsupial looked rather like a wolf but had tigerlike stripes on its lower body. It was once prolific throughout the whole of Australia but lost out in the battle for a single ecological niche to the dingo, surviving into historical times only in Tasmania. Here it met extinction thanks to the destructive incursions of the White man, a fate shared by the indigenous human race of Tasmanians. Over the past few decades, however, there have been a few isolated reports of sightings, and it may be that there is still a minuscule population of the creatures left in the island's more inaccessible regions. The fact that the Tasmanian tiger is nocturnal would assist in its remaining largely undetected.

**BELOW** A rare surviving photograph of the thylacine, or Tasmanian tiger. It is easy to see why the creature is sometimes called the Tasmanian wolf.

The Tasmanian tiger is one suspect in the quest for the identity of the Queensland tiger. The early settlers in Australia were unsurprised to discover that there was a marsupial equivalent of the tiger, and it was only when zoologists moved in to examine the wildlife of the "new" continent that the trouble started. By 1871–2 there was some interest in the fact that such an important member of the Australian ecosystem could have gone for so long unrecognized by zoology. The debate started when Brinsley G. Sheridan of Rockingham Bay, Queensland, passed on to the *Proceedings* an account given by his 13-year-old son:

> As big as a native Dog; its face was round like that of a Cat, it had a long tail, and its body was striped from the ribs under the belly with yellow and black. My Dog flew at it, but it could throw him. When they were together I fired my pistol at its head; the blood came. The animal then ran up a leaning tree, and the Dog barked at it. It then got savage and rushed down the tree at the Dog and then at me. I got frightened and came home.

Many of the individuals observed during the 19th century and in the first couple of decades of the 20th were about the size of a large dog, although one, shot near Tiaro in 1915 while suckling its kits, was only about the size of a wildcat and thus might have been thought to be an example of the indigenous creature called the tiger cat were it not for the fact that tiger cats are, confusingly, spotted rather than striped. Despite this and a couple of other similar reports, the general consensus is that the beast is a fairly hefty size; possibly there are two quite distinct unknown creatures involved, one of them being nothing more out-landish than a rare striped variety of tiger cat. Whatever the case, reports have dwindled in recent years (although at the same time they have become geographically more widely spread), and this would accord with the notion that an already much depleted population of the creature is today approaching extinction.

As noted, the Tasmanian tiger is a tempting candidate for being the Queensland tiger, yet the shape of the head is quite wrong: the Queensland creature is consistently described as having a flattish, feline face whereas that of the Tasmanian tiger is more typically lupine. The cryptozoological vote therefore goes instead to a creature otherwise known only from fossils and generally regarded as having become extinct 10,000 or more years ago. This is the marsupial lion, *Thylacoleo carnifex*, carnivorous member of what is otherwise a herbivorous group of mammals. The lack of more recent fossils need not be taken to preclude the animal's having survived until today, for 10,000 years is no time at all in palaeontological terms, especially should a creature's habitat be somewhere that good fossils rarely form and where, as a consequence, palaeontologists rarely go. Such a habitat is a rain forest, and indeed all the major centres for tiger sightings have been near rain forests, which would certainly support the hypothesis. The clincher would be the discovery of a skull, because the dentition of the marsupial lion (vastly enlarged incisors to compensate for almost nonexistent canines) is very distinctive.

## THE MOA

New Zealand is the home of the moa, a flightless and possibly fleet-footed bird that was until quite recently universally assumed to have become extinct through being hunted down by the Maoris, who immigrated to the islands from (probably) the Cook Islands around AD1350. Looking not unlike ostriches, moas stood up to 3m (10ft) tall; some were much smaller, yet one more recent witness, a man called George Pauley in 1823, said that the bird he encountered (both it and he promptly fled) was a staggering 6m (20ft) tall, but the size discrepancy could be put down to an exaggeration born of fear. An 1878 newspaper account tells what may have been a purely apocryphal story of a farmer who had seen strange tracks around his farm on numerous occasions. Since the newspaper gave no corroborative details, this tale was for long dismissed as merely one of the countless examples of fictional journalism that have always littered the world's newspapers. Nevertheless, in recent years the press has begun once more to carry occasional stories describing fleeting encounters with presumed moas, and so it is possible that some of the birds still survive.

To those who say that it is impossible for such an obvious member of the ecosystem to exist undetected on a populous island for several centuries, Bernard Heuvelmans has responded that exactly this happened in Bermuda, where the Bermuda petrel – not as large but, being flighted, every bit as obvious – was "lost" for some three centuries.

**BELOW** An artist's impression of the giant moa, with kiwis shown to give an impression of scale. The moa is generally believed to be extinct, but reports of sightings still occasionally trickle in.

# CREATURES LARGE AND SMALL

### ATHOL

Java is said to be the home of another anomalous flying creature, the athol, a huge batlike beast with a wingspan claimed to be as great as 3.75m (12ft 4in); it has grey fur and a face resembling that of a monkey. This would make the creature a little over twice the size of any formally recognized bat; moreover, the larger known bats have quite marked snouts, unlike their much smaller, flat-faced insectivorous cousins. The size and the facial shape, plus the lack of any bats of intermediate size, would seem to militate against the existence of the athol, but the fauna of the region is incompletely known.

### BURU

Asia is the claimed home also for a species of giant aquatic lizard, about the size of a big Komodo dragon (a lizard itself not definitively confirmed to exist until 1910). Called the buru, this seems to have run to about 4.5m (15ft) in length and to have been, despite its crocodilian size and appearance, herbivorous and dangerous to human beings only if trapped. According to the people in the valley of the Apu Tanis in the Himalayas – Yeti country – this beast was prolific during their ancestors' time although infrequently seen, as it spent almost all of its time in the water. As agriculture spread, the beasts became a nuisance, and were finally exterminated. Or were they? Some accounts suggest that a vastly diminished population of burus still survives in this and one or two neighbouring valleys. The region is sufficiently remote that no one is quite sure if indeed the buru still lives or, conversely, if it was never anything more than a legend.

### THE TAZELWÜRM

The Alps were widely believed during the early decades of this century to be the home of a rather smaller mystery lizard, the tazelwürm. The descriptions are far from unanimous, but it seems that the tazelwürm is a four-legged, heavy-bodied lizard, about 60–100cm (2–3ft) in length, and that in recent historical times its population in the region was plentiful. It has sometimes been compared with the Buru.

### THE SIRRUSH

Evidence for the beast, the sirrush was first uncovered in 1902, during the excavation of the Gate of Ishtar on the site of ancient Babylon. Depicted in one of the reliefs on the gate was a rather graceful-looking creature with a long neck, a scale-covered body, a single-horned head and a forked tongue; most intriguingly of all, its rear feet are like those of a bird while its forefeet much more closely resemble those of a large cat. The mixture of features would normally suggest one of the many mythical portmanteau creatures found in ancient depictions all over the world, but the animals portrayed around the sirrush are certainly not mythical – indeed, one that was originally regarded as such was later shown to be the urus, a now-extinct species of wild cow. The science writer and occasional cryptozoologist Willy Ley (1906–69) suggested that the combination of scales and birdlike feet might suggest some form of dinosaur; he seems not to have been much convinced by his own argument, though he does point out that in the Bible there is mention of the ancient Babylonions possessing a dragonlike animal.

## MOKÉLE-MBÊMBE

The last of the dinosaurs? The mind rebels against the notion of such a species surviving nearly 70 million years beyond the time at which its fellows perished and throughout that time leaving no fossil evidence at all. Exactly the same stricture applies to another putative African dinosaur, the mokéle-mbêmbe (known also under various other names, including chipekwe, amali, dingonek, ol-umaina and jago-nini). Since the late 19th century there have been tales of such a creature, a vast lizard-like beast dwelling in the swamps of central Africa. The descriptions given differ greatly in their details, and many of them seem as if they are of nothing more obscure than a crocodile. Other descriptions suggest a hugely vast hippopotamus, albeit with reptilian characteristics, or even something akin to a small brontosaur. That such a beast could survive might be indicated by the fact that the crocodile species itself has survived since the time of the dinosaurs and without gross evolutionary alteration. The idea of a pygmy brontosaur was supported by investigative expeditions to central Africa in 1980 and 1981 led by Roy P. Mackal. They interviewed a number of supposed eyewitnesses and inferred a composite description of a brownish creature about 10m (33ft) long, with a long neck – about one-third of the total length – and a small, combed head, a long, tapering tail and a semi-aquatic lifestyle; when out of the water it stood on four short legs.

## THE NANDI BEAR

A ferocious reported animal from nearby Kenya is the chemosit or Nandi bear. Much of the evidence suggests a macabre further sophistication of the creature's feeding habits: it cracks open the skulls and devours only the brains of its victims. Dr Charles Andrews (1866–1924) of London's Natural History Museum observed that the creature's appearance sounded to be not unlike that of a chalicotherium, a recently extinct mammal whose remains have been found on Samos in conjunction with those of the samotherium, a close cousin of the okapi. If the two animals could have shared a habitat on Samos, might they not equally happily do likewise in Africa? The hypothesis might seem to be disqualified by the fact that the chalicotherium was exclusively herbivorous; but if the vicious crimes perpetrated against humanity by hyenas, baboons, ratels and other human beings are married to the doubtless terrifying appearance of the chalicotherium, it is possible that, as is so often the case, it is the least guilty of the creatures that is made the scapegoat for the crimes of the others.

### THE MEGATHERIUM

The modern tree sloth of South America is a comparatively small, reclusive creature of notoriously lazy habits. It represents the sole surviving strain of a rich diversity of sloths that inhabited the vast area of Patagonia until about the end of the last glacial period of the Pleistocene Ice Age, some 12,000 years ago; these varied in size from that of the tree sloth up to that of an elephant. This last beast, megatherium, was first reconstructed in 1796 (from an assemblage of bones discovered in 1789) by the Spanish naturalist José Garriga and first taxonomically classified by the French anatomist Georges Cuvier (1769–1832), who christened it *Megatherium*, a Latin name meaning nothing more imaginative than "large mammal". Standing on its hind legs the beast must have reared to about 5m (16ft 6in) in height. Until late in the 19th century it was believed that these South American monsters could never have been encountered by human beings.

Evidence began to emerge that a number of the giant edentates (of which megatherium is/was one) were still extant. The cause was championed by Florentino Ameghino, who came across what seemed to be concrete proof that something much like the mylodon (a fossil edentate similar to the megatherium but smaller – about the size of an ox – and with a much longer tail) was still alive; the first evidence came to him in the form of a collection of bean-sized bones that had been dug out of a thick animal skin, a natural mode of protection typical of all the ground sloths. Ameghino's instincts (one cannot say his professional judgement) told him that this must have come from a creature much like the one that his friend Ramon Lista had described encountering some years earlier: this had been less than 1.5m (5ft) long, which is a lot smaller than the average ox, but could easily have been, Ameghino decided, a mylodon that was not yet fully grown. Certainly Lista's description of how the beast had been unconcerned by being shot accorded with the notion that its skin was tough and internally armoured by bones.

It is a long leap from a pig-sized creature such as Lista described to the vast megatherium, and even to the ox-sized mylodon. Nevertheless, further discoveries increased the probability that such a beast as mylodon did indeed survive. While others were making these finds, Ameghino was approaching the problem from a different angle: he was looking for further evidence in the accounts left by early travellers to the New World. Among these, in a vast work published in 1740–46 by the Portuguese Jesuit Pedro Lozano, he came across reference to a terrifying giant beast, which the Paraguayan natives had called the succarath (or su). This was hunted for its skin, from which cloaks were made. The succarath,

## MEGATHERIUM

Lozano noted, carried its young on its back, a behaviour typical of anteaters and sloths.

The succarath would seem almost certainly to have been some sort of large ground sloth, and it appears that there were still such beings extant into the 16th century – hardly longer ago than yesterday when we're talking about beasts that were supposed to have been extinct 12,000 years ago.

## THE IEMISCH

*In Argentina the monster that is regarded with most horror as an inveterate man-killer is the iemisch or hymché, a beast that bears many resemblances to the tiger but has webbed feet as befits its largely aquatic lifestyle. Carlos Ameghino, brother of the prominent Argentinian palaeontologist and champion of megatherium (see page 48) Professor Florentino Ameghino, in 1897 sent his brother a few little bones supposed to come from this creature. His accompanying explanation ran in part:*

> *This animal is of nocturnal habits, and it is said to be so strong that it can seize horses with its claws and drag them to the bottom of the water. According to the description I have been given, it has a short head, big canine teeth, and no external ears; its feet are short and plantigrade, with three toes on the forefeet and four on the hind; these toes are joined by a membrane for swimming, and are also armed with formidable claws. Its tail is long, flat and prehensile. Its body is covered with short hair, coarse and stiff, of a uniform bay colour. In size it is said to be larger than a puma, but its paws are shorter and its body thicker.*

*Florentino Ameghino claimed this beast as another example of megatherium, the giant sloth, even going so far in his own accounts as to alter the number of toes as given by Carlos. In fact, whatever the iemisch is, it most certainly is not a giant sloth. Cryptozoologists are divided on the issue, but many believe that it must be some unknown species of giant otter; a variant of the theory is that stories have conflated two known beasts of the area, the otter, which is aquatic, and the jaguar, which can certainly be appropriately vicious.*

**LEFT** An artist's impression of *Megatherium,* the giant ground sloth. Although the animal is widely regarded as having become extinct some thousands of years ago, there are persistent reports of it and other giant edentates having been sighted in the remote areas of South America.

# MONSTROUS SNAKES

## THE ANACONDA

South America is also the home of various giant snakes. Reports of varying veracity talk of anacondas of colossal length, sizes like 22.5m (74ft) and even 40m (131ft) being occasionally given. Even though the longest properly authenticated anaconda, killed in Brazil around 1960, was only 8.45m (27ft 9in) long, that is still no mean snake. Bernard Heuvelmans, in *On the Track of Unknown Animals*, recounts a telling story. When he asked the French painter Serge Bonacase, who in 1947 had witnessed in Brazil the shooting of an anaconda whose length was estimated by Bonacase at 22.5m (74ft), why the Europeans in the party had not thought to bring home the skull or skin as proof of their claims, Bonacase replied that the Brazilians seemed so unsurprised that the Europeans assumed that snakes of this size were commonplace.

Perhaps rather confusingly named is the giant boa, an aquatic rather than a terrestrial serpent. Most of the descriptions have come to us through the efforts of a priest, Victor Heinz, who after twice having encountered such creatures became passionately interested in them, interviewing other eyewitnesses in the course of his researches. According to many of these reports, one peculiarity of the colossal water serpents is that their large eyes are phosphorescent; indeed, it is believed that their habit of seeming to attack river steamers is because they mistake the lights of the craft for the eyes of their fellows, and rush forward either in a display of territorial aggression or as an amorous gambit.

## THE MIÑHOCÃO

A rather different beast is the miñhocão which, while similarly enormous, seems to be not so much a snake as a worm – "worm" in the sense of the gigantic, destructive and sinister creatures encountered in European folklore. Other theories are that it might be some sort of giant burrowing armadillo, perhaps a surviving glyptodon, even though it is reported to be semi-aquatic, which armadillos are not; the burrow left by a creature like this would certainly look as if it could equally well have been carved out by a worm. The champion of this creature's existence was a German embryologist resident in Brazil, one Fritz Müller (1821–97), who was as engrossed with it as Victor Heinz was later to be with the giant boa. His views were written up in the 21 February 1878 issue of *Nature* and included a number of accounts of encounters that various of his interviewees had described to him.

An artist's dramatic impression
of one of the great snakes believed to threaten travellers on the rivers of
Paraguay and other South American countries.

# CHAPTER THREE

# THE LITTLE PEOPLE

## FAIRIES

Between 1917 and 1920 two young girls, Frances Griffiths and her cousin, Elsie Wright, took a series of photographs in a "fairy glen" at the back of Elsie's house in Yorkshire, England. These photographs purported to show the girls playing with elves and fairies – who came complete with wings and puckish expressions, just like the ones

painted by Walter Crane and others for Victorian children's books. Sir Arthur Conan Doyle (1859–1930), whose interest in matters psychic was intense, helped to publicize the case, and the affair of the Cottingley Fairies has become established in the literature. Our ancestors marvelled, and it is still frequently said that no scientific test has been able to prove that these photographs were faked. This faith in them is curious, because a brief look reveals sufficient discrepancies of focus and perspective to indicate that the fairies are (beautifully rendered) paper cut-outs – as the two hoaxers themselves confessed in later life. Reminding ourselves that the science of photography was still in its youth when the Cottingley pictures were taken, we must recall David Langford's declamatory remark in the conclusion to his UFO hoax, *An Account of a Meeting with Denizens of Another World*, 1871: "I can only declare that the manuscript has so far withstood every test of authenticity to which it has been subjected." (The prominent ufologist Whitley Strieber, citing the "case" in *Majestic*, paraphrased this as: "The ms. has been authenticated by British antiquarians." This may hint at another reason for the persistence of the Cottingley Faith myth.)

A further reason for doubting the photographs had always been that the idea of fairies as ethereal miniatures is a comparatively recent one. The Little People – elementals – were traditionally regarded as something rather different: they were troglodytic spirits, about the size of a 10-year-old human child; and, far from being friendly and playful, they could be very unpleasant indeed if crossed. They possessed formidable spiritual powers and a considerable erotic charge, and some varieties had extremely nasty habits – redcaps, for example, got their name from their practice of dyeing their caps in the blood of unfortunate travellers, and the *baobhan sith* took the form of beautiful women in order to capture the love of men, whom they then sucked dry of their blood. (This latter characteristic is almost identical with that of the *lamia*; see page 86.) Leprechauns and brownies, who were positively helpful to human beings, were very much in the minority. More typically, even those fairies who were comparatively amicable were quick to take offence, snobbish (they insisted on being referred to as "gentry") and likely to steal a human baby, replacing it with one of their own (a changeling). Only cajolery or bribery could elicit the benefits they could confer – hence the practice of leaving out a saucerful of milk on the windowsill overnight.

**LEFT** One of the famous series of faked photographs of the "Cottingley Fairies", taken between 1917 and 1920 by two Yorkshire schoolgirls. In later life, the two protagonists confessed to their childhood fraud, but the photographs are still occasionally treated as if genuine.

## OBERON AND TITANIA

The King and Queen of the Little People were, as in Shakespeare's *A Midsummer Night's Dream* (*c*.595), Oberon and Titania. According to one legend of the former, he became a great friend and exceptionally useful ally of Huon de Bordeaux, a hero-vassal who played a part in the cluster of legends surrounding Charlemagne, and told him of his parentage. In the words of Brewer (1894 edn), this "humpty dwarf, only three feet high, but of angelic face" told Huon that

> The lady of the Hidden Isle (Cephalonia) married Neptanebus, King of Egypt, by whom she had a son called Alexander the Great. Seven hundred years later Julius Caesar, on his way to Thessaly, stopped in Cephalonia, and the same lady, falling in love with him, had in time another son, and that son was Oberon. At his birth the fairies bestowed their gifts – one was insight into men's thoughts, and another was the power of transporting himself to any place instantaneously . . . In the fullness of time, falling asleep in death, legions of angels conveyed his soul to Paradise.

**BELOW** Oberon and Titania, the king and queen of Fairyland. A 19th-century print after a painting by Noel Paton showing a scene from Shakespeare's *A Midsummer Night's Dream.*

**LEFT** **A fairy ring, as depicted in Olaus Magnus'** *Historia de Gentibus Septentrionalibus* **(1558). Both this picture and that of Robin Goodfellow (page 56) demonstrate a very different view of the fairies from that in the Cottingley fakes. Note in particular the phallic (fertility) imagery, here expressed by the serpent in the hand of the dancer on the left.**

Whoever was responsible for the legend clearly regarded the Little People as being humanlike in many ways: not only were they mortal and favoured by God's love, they were capable of interbreeding with humans. Oberon's wife, Titania, appears to be either a later or an earlier immigrant to Fairyland, depending on one's viewpoint: she can be equated with the Greek goddess Diana, who was in fact referred to as Titania (along with Latona, Pyrrha and Circe as descendants of the Titans) by Ovid, but her incarnation as the Queen of Fairyland seems to have begun not long before Shakespeare was writing about her.

And then there were the very nasty elementals. The nuckelavee of the Scottish Lowlands had a head 10 times the size of that of a man, no skin, a piglike mouth and such corrosive halitosis that its breath could shrivel crops and debilitate or even destroy domesticated animals. The kelpie, a malevolent water spirit, used to take the form of a handsome young man or, more typically, a splendid horse; travellers would be offered carriage across a stretch of water, any of them gullible enough to accept the proposal being drowned and devoured. Yet kelpies, like unicorns, could be drawn by beautiful maidens, who would put on them a bridle whose halter had a cross cut out of it; the kelpie would then remain tame and could be persuaded to perform everyday duties.

It may seem that such whimsical discussion is a long way from monster-hunting, but this estimation is born of our own era, when we have become inured to the gauzy-winged, cutie-pie image of the fairy spawned not only by the Victorians but also by the 20th century media, perhaps most notably the figure of Tinkerbell created by Disney for the movie *Peter Pan* (1953). We forget that, to our ancestors, the Little People were very real indeed; moreover, the whole elaborate construction of Fairyland may have had a far more solid factual basis than modern rationalism might care to admit.

## PIXIES

The son of Oberon and his Queen was Robin Goodfellow, who dressed ever in green; he may have been the source for the legends about Robin Hood, although more likely there was a conflation of legends, since a certain amount of evidence exists to suggest that there is some independent factual basis for the Robin Hood mythos. Robin Goodfellow's alter ego, Puck, is a name related to the word "pook", meaning an elf or sprite; this word can be related to the Dutch spook, the Icelandic piki, the Irish pooka and the Welsh puca, and possibly also to the Swedish pysk, which gives us the word "pixie". It is feasible that a dimunitive of Robin Goodfellow's first name became the "hob" of "hobgoblin", the corruption coming via "Rob-Goblin", meaning "Rob the Goblin"; hobgoblins were generally regarded as anything from mischievous to dire, the worst variety of them all being the imps which, in an interesting linkage with primitive Judaeo-Christian tradition, came from Hell – i.e., they were cognate with demons. In place of hands, imps had naked feet; they also had devilish tails. The word "elf" really just means the same as "fairy", coming from an Anglo-Saxon word for "spirit"; however, elves came to be regarded as the louts of fairyland, with tempers and manners even worse than those of their fellows.

**LEFT** An illustration from a 17th-century tract showing Robin Goodfellow (often equated with Puck), the son of Oberon and Titania.

## WERE THEY REAL?

According to one theory, there did indeed exist alongside humanity a species of intelligent, humanoid (although on average smaller) creatures. The relationship between the two species would have been guarded although not necessarily hostile, much like that between the different peoples of humankind today. Unlike the case with modern racism, however, any tension between the two species would have had at its core some reasonable cause, for naturally the two would have been in pursuit of the same ecological niche (a point discussed more fully in the context of werewolves on page 88) – indeed, it shows surprising tolerance on the part of the two species that they did not simply attempt to annihilate each other. Even so, the weaker and less populous of the two species died out over the centuries, so that today they are completely forgotten except in folk-tales – unless, of course, there are still a few isolated survivors hiding away in secluded places.

What, then, might this secondary species have been? There are two ways in which it could have been the Neanderthals. First, we know that our Cro-Magnon ancestors coexisted and intermingled with the Neanderthals in many parts of Europe; until quite recently it was believed that the Cro-Magnons simply exterminated the mentally and technologically inferior species, but it is now apparent that the extinction came about more through a sort of cultural attrition. The relationship between Cro-Magnon and Neanderthal must have been very much like the hypothetical one posited above between humans and fairies. The Neanderthals became extinct over 10–15,000 years ago, but memories can be preserved for astonishingly long periods via the oral tradition. Even so, 10–15,000 years is probably stretching things a little.

A superficially more attractive possibility is that the Neanderthals survived until a very much later date than we generally recognize – indeed, that they still be among us, having become absorbed into the general human population in much the same way as, for example, the Ainu have merged into the mainstream Japanese stock. It is perfectly feasible that at least until the Dark Ages and possibly later there were quite genuinely "little people" sharing the land with their larger, more aggressive cousins. In more cultivated areas they might long since have disappeared, but in the more remote parts of northern Europe they could well have clung on, less threatened by the tramp of civilization and by peoples whose relationship with nature had not been too sullied

by brute rationalism – that is, who were prepared to accept the "others" as a fact of life rather than regard them as something "unnatural" and therefore to be annihilated.

This hypothesis is, of course, damaged by the lack of fossil evidence, although it would be fair to point out that we would be unlikely to notice any characteristics of the Neanderthal in skeletons a mere thousand or so years old because we would not be looking for them. In the hypothesis's favour, however, is the fact that many of the inferred traits of Neanderthal society and psychology are uncannily like those attributed to the fairies. If Neanderthal modes of thought were governed more by the right brain than by the left (loosely speaking, more by the intuitive than the analytical parts of the consciousness), something we may conjecture on the basis of the scant physical evidence left behind by the Neanderthal cultures (that scantness itself is a further basis for the speculation), then to the more down-to-earth human main-stock their little cousins might well have displayed an overall pattern of behaviour that we can describe, quite accurately, as feyness. Some of the intuitive abilities of the Neanderthals, being beyond the comprehension of the analytical Cro-Magnon mind, would have seemed quite magical. The loric knowledge of herbal medicine would have been a science far beyond the scope of the Cro-Magnon's technological worldview. In his thought-provoking *Cities of Dreams*, Stan Gooch takes a rather similar argument much further than we have space for here, and the interested reader is urged to consult that book.

BELOW **The dwarfs of German folklore were typically ill tempered craftsmen; the most famous examples are of course the Nibelungen, as featured in Wagner's Ring Cycle.**

# LITTLE GREEN MEN

A quite separate theory links the various denizens of Fairyland to what can be generically termed Little Green Men, or LGMs. These are the purported occupants of UFOs, and they need be neither little nor green (most certainly, of course, they are not men). The expression "UFOs", rather than "flying saucers", is used advisedly here, because when we talk of LGMs we are not necessarily implying that the creatures reported are extraterrestrial visitors – nor, indeed, that they have any physical existence at all. Most sober ufologists today give little credence to theories that UFOs are craft of any kind, whether from distant planets, the future or alternate universes, although none of these hypotheses is inherently impossible; rather, they are interested in the UFO experience as a psychological or parapsychological phenomenon. This distinction between the two "branches" of ufology is quite an important one, although not always obvious to the outsider. One major reason for the confusion is that the popular media rarely differentiate between the responsible ufologists and the crazies, most of whom are fanatical supporters of the "extraterrestrial hypothesis" (although some of the supporters of this hypothesis are perfectly responsible). A second major reason is that the crazies, being richer (sensationalism pays better), have in recent years got into the habit of using the law to stifle the dissenting voices of the responsible researchers, thereby, through their obvious ignorance of the debate that fuels scientific progress, betraying the non-science of their working methods. So, although we shall treat LGMs as if they were real, physical monsters, it should be borne in mind that this is for the purposes of simplicity only: they have reality, but not necessarily in the sense that we would normally use that term.

It is almost certainly the case that each succeeding age and each culture produces its own cluster of "supernatural objects", whose characteristics are somehow in tune with the *Zeitgeist*. The history of ufology, and of the presumed occupants of the presumed craft, is an object-lesson in this sort of cultural evolution. Explanations for perceived lights in the sky go back a very long way; we can draw analogies with the radiant auras of angels and the shining haloes of the revered. It seems likely that the author of *Ezekiel* was describing the rare atmospheric phenomenon of "sundogs" ("additional suns" ringing the Sun, and joined to it by spokes of light) when he wrote, in *i*, 4–27:

BELOW **A possible UFO entity – one of the 20th century's Little People – photographed by Police Chief Jeff Greenshaw at Falkville, Alabama, on 17th October 1973.**

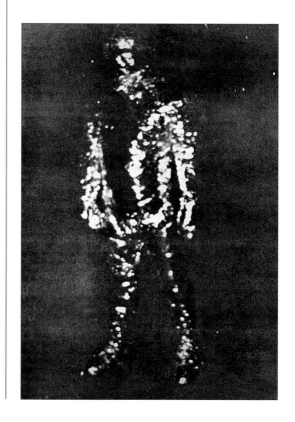

**BELOW An artist's impression of an alien spacecraft alleged to have landed in the back yard of chicken farmer Joe Simonton on the outskirts of Eagle River, Wisconsin, on 18th April 1961. The occupants of the craft paused long enough to make themselves some pancakes, three of which they gave to Simonton; on analysis these proved to be made of perfectly terrestrial ingredients. The story might be dismissed as a preposterous invention were it not for what is at least an interesting coincidence. The fairies of Ireland were often said to live on pancakes; moreover, they had a habit of introducing themselves to mortals with a gift of food.**

And I looked, and, behold, a whirlwind came out of the north, a great cloud, and a fire unfolding itself, and a brightness was about it, and out of the midst thereof as the colour of amber, out of the midst of the fire.

Also out of the midst thereof came the likeness of four living creatures. And this was their appearance; they had the likeness of a man.

And every one had four faces, and every one had four wings.

And their feet were straight feet; and the sole of their feet was like the sole of a calf's foot: and they sparkled like the colour of burnished brass.

And when they went, I heard the noise of their wings, like the noise of great waters, as the voice of the Almighty, the voice of speech, as the voice of a host: when they stood, they let down their wings . . . .

And I saw as the colour of amber, as the appearance of fire round about within it, from the appearance of his loins even upward, and from the appearance of his loins even downward, I saw as it were the appearance of fire, and it had brightness round about.

All of this may seem an astonishingly elaborate structure to found upon the witnessing of an atmospheric phenomenon, no matter how spectacular, yet it is probably the best eyewitness account of a sighting of supernatural monsters ever penned. One can guess that it is reliable in every detail: the writer saw exactly what he says he saw; nowhere did

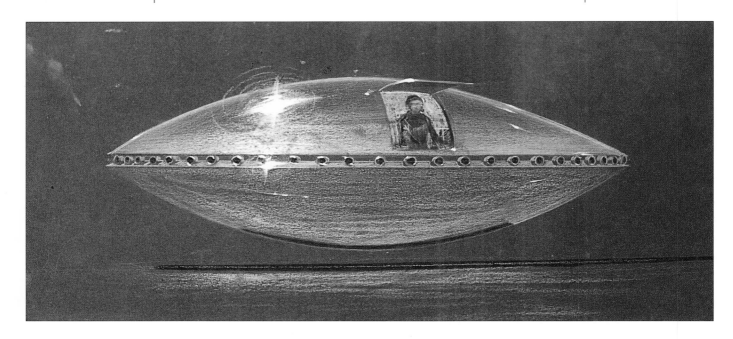

he fall into the temptation of invoking poetic licence. The description is the absolute, literal, word-for-word truth of what the author witnessed. It has been suggested that the writer was recalling the Assyrian *karibu*, statues of animals with human heads that guarded the palace at Ninevan.

It is *not*, however, a good description of what a late-20th century human being, born into and acclimatized to a technological culture, would have seen. Such an individual might have witnessed a rare and impressive atmospheric phenomenon or, possibly, a flight of flying saucers. In an earlier age, a similar observer might have seen, quite distinctly, a flight of angels or of witches and have described them, with total honesty, down to the last detail of their wings or broomsticks. By the end of the 19th century, however, observers were more objective . . . weren't they?

Over the winter and spring of 1896–7, North America was bewildered by reports of airships. At that time the airship was regarded in much the same way that we regard shuttle-type spaceships today: although we don't think of them as being in any way supernatural, we would, unless we lived in certain parts of the USA, be pretty startled if one flew overhead. The mysterious airship more or less crossed the USA from west to east, taking five months over the journey. It was "seen" by countless people, some of whom were certainly hoaxers; hoaxers also entered the picture more directly by carrying out pranks such as sending up hot-air balloons. A number of people came forward to claim personal acquaintanceship with the airship's inventors, giving details as to its design and destination. The considerate crew of the craft even dropped letters overboard, one of them addressed to Thomas Alva Edison (1847–1931). In fact, it was Edison's public denunciation of the whole affair that brought the case to an end: sightings abruptly stopped.

The parallels with modern UFO "flaps" need hardly be pointed out. What was originally, no doubt, a case of mistaken identification of some aerial phenomenon was blown up out of all proportion by word-of-mouth retelling and, of course, by the enthusiastic efforts of the media. From then on, for the next few months, whenever there was a strange light in the sky its observers – and not just the more gullible among them – were able, as their eyes strained to make out detail, to see an airship. On occasion they were even able to make out the silhouettes of the crew against the airship's lighted portholes. When they described what they had witnessed, they were telling the literal truth – the literal truth, rather than the objective truth.

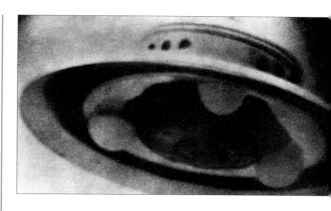

**ABOVE** The underside of a UFO photographed by the most famous contactee of all, soft-drinks salesman George Adamski, in 1952. Sceptics have suggested that this interstellar craft looks remarkably like the top of a particular type of soft-drinks cooler.

## 20TH-CENTURY SIGHTINGS

In our modern era, we see spaceships – especially since 1947, when Kenneth Arnold saw the first set of "flying saucers". We don't see crew-members looking down at us from lighted portholes: we see LGMs.

### LGMs (LITTLE GREEN MEN)

*LGMs are very rarely green: that coloration seems to have been imported into sensationalist accounts from pulp science fiction. Ufonauts seem to fall into a number of quite distinct species, leading the supporters of the extraterrestrial hypothesis to conclude that we are under observation by explorers from a similar number of other worlds. The commonest species is humanoid; its members stand about 1.4m (4ft 7in) tall and their skin is usually described as white or grey in colour and sometimes as scaly. Their arms reach down to their knees; their hands may have fewer digits than the human hand. Their large heads are bald all over; their eyes are elongated-almond-shaped; their chins are pointed; their mouths are slits; lthey have nostrils but,* *usually, no noses as such. They dress in tight-fitting, single-piece garments of a single, bland colour. Rather than walk, they float or glide. Communication between them and with those humans they meet is by telepathy.*

*Other varieties are less common. Members of one are tall, fair-haired, good-looking and sufficiently like ourselves to mix undetected in human company. Members of another look like Bigfoot. Members of yet another are small, hairy and aggressive, their hands armed with claws. Sometimes the ufonauts are robots. And, finally, there are the rare green ones . . .*

These were first encountered a few months after Arnold's pioneering experience by an artist called Rapuzzi Luigi Johannis, who was hiking in the wilds on the Italian-Yugoslav border; he claimed later that at the time he knew nothing of the sighting by Arnold that had set the media world ablaze. He came across a bright red spheroid, some 3m (10ft) in diameter, with a couple of figures standing beside it; in the few seconds before he registered the greenness of their skin, he assumed them to be small boys, of height less than a metre (3ft 3½in). They were dressed in brown and wore close-fitting caps, which may or may not have concealed hair – probably not, because their faces were entirely hairless. All in all, although smaller and green in colour, they were otherwise very like the common grey ufonauts described above. For some reason, Johannis waved his geologist's pick at them, and they knocked him to the ground using some sort of hi-tech stun-weapon; as he lay there gasping, they swiped his pick, boarded the sphere and flew away silently.

**ABOVE Artist's impression of one of the Hopkinsville goblins at work in Kentucky in 1955.**

Perhaps also green are the pathetic little corpses supposedly stored away in a freezer by the US authorities after a UFO crashed in the 1940s. Further discussion of this, the MJ–12 ("Majestic") affair, is not possible here for legal reasons. It does seem safe to mention, however, that autopsies have shown that the aliens had, in life, a predilection for strawberry ice-cream.

One of the best early cases of a close encounter with LGMs occurred in 1955 in Kelly-Hopkinsville, Kentucky, on the farmstead of a family called Sutton; the creatures observed were of the common variety, with protuberant yellow eyes, except that they had prominent, pointed ears. The house had visitors at the time, so there were plenty of witnesses – eight adults and three children. The incident began at about 7.00pm when a son of the family went outside to fetch a drink from the well. On his return he remarked that he had seen what looked like a bright object landing nearby; both the remark and the reaction to it seem to have been casual. But an hour or so later one of the dogs began barking frenziedly, and the company, alerted, saw that a little glowing humanoid was walking towards the house, its hands in the air. Presumably on the age-tested principle that the only good member of a starfaring civilization is a dead member of a starfaring civilization, a couple of the men shot at it, despite the raised hands, whereupon it did a somersault and vanished into the darkness. Then another humanoid showed its face at the window. Someone shot it, right through the glass and seemed to injure it, although not so seriously that it wasn't able to make its escape. Soon the Suttons and their guests found that there was no question of the LGM having been injured: as they went outside to look for the body, they saw several others (although never more than two at once), and demonstrated empirically that the creatures were impervious to bullets, which just bounced off them. But the LGMs apparently did have one vulnerability: their eyes seemed to be inordinately light-sensitive. By 11.00pm the group had had enough and packed into their cars to drive to the police station in Hopkinsville. The police took the party's excited claims to have been attacked by glowing bug-eyed goblins seriously, and officers were sent to investigate. As they approached the farm they saw a number of lights rising into the sky, and one of the officers later said he heard two of these whooshing overhead. At the farm the police found lots of bullet-holes and the like, but no other evidence of an alien presence.

## THE HILL STORY

The Kelly-Hopkinsville incident has never been satisfactorily explained in mundane terms. The most famous of all the encounters with similar beings has, however, probably been so: the case is that of Betty and Barney Hill, popularized in John Fuller's 1966 book, *The Interrupted Journey*. There is no question of hoaxing having been involved in this incident. In 1961 the Hills were driving back to their home in Portsmouth, New Hampshire, when they saw a light in the sky: they thought it might be a spaceship. When they reached home they discovered that somehow they had "lost" a couple of hours. Then Betty began having dreams about being examined by alien beings aboard their spacecraft. Later, under hypnosis, she told of exactly this having happened during those "lost" hours. Barney, also under hypnosis, confirmed her story. The light they had seen was a collection of flashing, coloured lights, which had moved erratically across the sky, and they had watched its progress for some while, on occasion using binoculars. When it finally came close to them, they stopped the car and saw a disc-shaped craft hovering no more than 20m (66ft) away from them; humanoid creatures regarded them briefly through the craft's windows, then all but one of these turned away towards what looked like a console. The craft smoothly came to ground, and soon after they were taken aboard the craft by

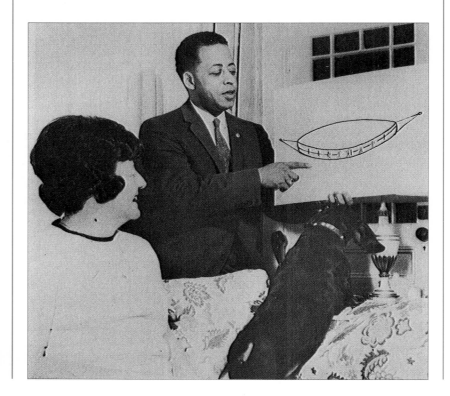

**RIGHT  Betty and Barney Hill who, it is claimed, were abducted by a UFO when driving home to Portsmouth, New Hampshire, in 1961.**

**LEFT** An artist's impression, based on accounts given under hypnosis by Betty and Barney Hill, of the faces of the aliens who they believed had abducted them.

telepathic, black-suited aliens who accorded in appearance with the common description, although Betty was particularly emphatic about their eyes, which apparently were so elongated that they wrapped around the sides of the head. There was no suggestion of any unfriendliness towards them on the part of the LGMs; indeed, one of them showed Betty a star-map in response to her question as to where the craft had come from, explaining to her that it didn't matter if she knew, because soon the memory of the incident would be wiped from her consciousness.

However, as a result of hypnosis, Betty was years later able to reproduce the star-map from memory. If regarded as being three-dimensional, it conformed to a hypothesis that the LGMs' home was a planet of the star Eta Reticuli, some 37 light years distant. However, for reasons that become evident after only a little thought, the same map could be made to "fit" with countless other patterns of nearby stars, depending on the orientation of the 3-D image, and especially since it did not come with a scale (and was anyway, being drawn from memory, only an approximation). Analysing the incident in *The UFO Enigma*, Donald H. Menzel and Ernest H. Taves tell how very similar maps can be created in profusion using a randon-number generator.

But what of the main story? Surely Betty and Barney, under separate hypnosis, could not have produced an identical tale? In fact, *pace* too many popular recitals of the incident, they didn't: there are many differences of detail, some of them quite significant ones, and there are also internal inconsistencies in the two versions. What appears to have happened is that they were indeed startled by a strangely behaving UFO: exactly what this was we shall probably never know, but the writer Philip Klass (b.1920; well known under his real name for his writings probing ufology and related issues, and also as William Tenn for his science fiction) has made a convincing case for a ball of plasma, akin to ball lightning, which might be expected in connection with the high-tension power line that runs beside the highway along which the Hills were travelling when the incident occurred. We can guess that, assuming that it was a UFO and terrified that they might be abducted, the Hills shot up a side-road and hid for a couple of hours, which action their quite genuine fear later wiped from their conscious minds. Not from their subconscious minds, however: Betty's subconscious, speaking in the typically confusing language of the right brain, amalgamated the experience with what she had read about UFOs and produced the dreams that plagued her. Naturally she told her husband of these, and he became persuaded that the dreams represented genuine memories, which he began, cloudily, to "remember" himself. (This may sound peculiar, but in fact the memory phenomenon of "reading back", as it is called, is very common indeed.) Barney's suggestibility would certainly have been enhanced (as the investigating psychologist reported) by the very strong bond between the Hills: their skins were of different colours, which inevitably created social and psychological stresses for them in the USA of the early 1960s, the result of which was an exceptionally steadfast loyalty between the two of them. Under hypnosis Betty recounted what she quite truthfully and fundamentally recalled having happened; Barney did likewise, but his "recollections" were at second-hand, as it were, and consequently differed in many particulars. Such, at least, was the conclusion of the investigating hypnotherapist, and there seems little reason to doubt his verdict.

**ABOVE A recent (1990) photograph of Betty Andreasson-Luca (*née* Andreasson). Her account of her abduction by UFOnauts in 1967 bears strong resemblances to the accounts, given in previous centuries, of excursions to Fairyland.**

## ABDUCTION IN MASSACHUSETTS

Another tale whose details were uncovered through regression hypnosis concerned the apparent abduction of Betty Andreasson of South Ashburnham, Massachusetts, in January, 1967. It is tempting to point out that this was only a few months after John Fuller's book had made the Hills internationally famous and to leave it at that, but in fact the incident was very different, although the LGMs were the same, right down to their wrap-around eyes. This time the uniforms were blue, rather than black, and bore a phoenix-like symbol.

The evening of 25 January started out much as usual for the Andreassons. Then there was a power failure, and all the lights went out. After a glow visible through the windows, the electric lights came back on, but now all the Andreassons were frozen into complete immobility with the exception of Betty. In came the LGMs; their leader introduced himself telepathically to her as Quazgaa and gave her a blue book – which vanished during the rest of the encounter – in exchange for a copy of the Bible. (Is it possible that there was some connection with the USAF's investigation, Project Blue Book, which ran in 1952–69?). Then she was escorted out of the house and into an oval-shaped saucer, where she was given a (painful) medical examination.

The next part of her story is astonishingly close to the myriad accounts of being taken to Fairyland that Stan Gooch has suggested were possibly the result of Neantherthal survivals treating their contemporaries to hallucinogens. Andreasson was briefly immersed in a fluid which gave her pleasant sensations when she breathed. The fluid gone, she was led through darkness to a place where everything was red and there were lemur-like creatures with eyes on stalks in place of heads; next she and her alien companions went to a place where all was green. She was confronted by a great bird, 4.5m (15ft) tall, incadescently backlit. The light flared, and when she was able to look once more the bird was gone, in its place a raging fire. A little later, there emerged from the ashes a big fat worm. At the same time someone or something – perhaps the worm, perhaps not (Andreasson, deeply religious, assumed it was God) – began to speak inside her head, telling her that she had been selected to perform a mission on Earth, details of which would be revealed to her in due course. Then she was taken back home, where the rest of her family were still frozen. Exhausted, she went to bed. When she woke on the morrow everybody else was going about their normal business, oblivious to what had happened. (Later, also under hypnosis, two of her family told stories which corroborated hers and seemed to indicate that they were partly aware of what was going on.)

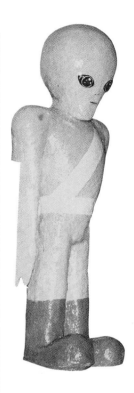

**ABOVE Model of Quazgaa, the leader of the aliens whom Betty Andreasson believed to have abducted her.**

ABOVE **Four of the six boys who in 1952 witnessed the infamous monster visitation near Flatwoods, West Virginia.**

Doubtless more than one sceptic has asked what it was that the Andreassons were smoking that night. The cynicism, although misplaced (the LGMs could hardly have picked a more sober, upstanding family), hints at a more interesting possibility. Hallucinogens do not create illusions in the mind: those illusions are already there, but are unperceived by us. In simple terms, we may say that the hallucinogen suppresses the activity of the analytical left brain and permits the usually suppressed right brain to display itself in its full unfiltered glory; since the right brain is not adept at speech but can communicate, any verbal component of a hallucination will seem to be in gibberish yet perfectly comprehensible, which is exactly the same effect as we would expect were an alient to talk to us both physically and telepathically at the same time. The taking of hallucinogens is not the only way to gain such access to the right brain: we do something similar when we dream.

## EXOTIC ALIENS

Moving to the more exotic monsters presumed to be alien visitors, we immediately encounter the creature seen by a group of two adults and six children on the evening of 12 September 1952 near the village of Flatwoods, West Virginia. The first thing to be seen was a swift-moving red object in the sky; it landed behind the brow of a small hill, and the sky was briefly lit up by a pulse of orange. On approaching the spot the humans noticed a noxious, spreading, ground-clinging mist; then they saw two great eyes glowing at them from the darkness of a nearby tree. One of the children pointed his torch in that direction, and the whole party saw a bulky, armless creature, about 3m (10ft) tall, staring at them. Its head was the shape of an inverted ace of spades; in the centre of this was a circular opening through which two large eyes shone with their own light. Further away the terrified humans could see what looked like some kind of spacecraft, shaped like an onion (i.e., again like an inverted ace of spades, but in three dimensions); this was pulsing in different colours from dull red to bright orange, as if there were something serious the matter with it. When the monster began to float across the ground towards them, the humans turned and fled.

Later that evening the local sheriff led a party to investigate the area, but in the poor light all they detected was a residual foul smell. The next day, however, it was possible to make out a circular patch of depressed ground, some 5m (16ft 6in) in diameter, at the place where the witnesses had said the spacecraft had been resting. Also, further witnesses now claimed that they, too, had seen a total of five bizarre and bizarrely behaving lights in the sky that evening at about the time

presidency of the USA under the aegis of the Universal Party, whose aim was to spread extraterrestrial wisdom among us; his running mate was Gabriel Green (b.1924), who had first begun to cock his hat towards the presidency in 1960 at the urging of a friend from one of the planets circling Alpha Centauri. That first time around Green withdrew, thus letting in John F. Kennedy.

A beautiful blonde lady from space met a certain Howard Menger in New England during his childhood, and later, during the 1950s, her kind came often to his home. Among the services he rendered to them was giving them haircuts so that they could, in those pre-hippie days, mingle more easily with the Earthlings. On one occasion they took him to the Moon, where the atmosphere was easily breathable. To quote Margaret Sachs in her highly recommended *The UFO Encyclopedia*:

> He brought back some lunar potatoes which reportedly contained five times the protein found in terrestrial potatoes. Their nutritive value could not be proved, however, because Menger had supposedly handed them over to the US Government, which was keeping them a secret.

Yet another cover-up! Reinhold Schmidt met countless human-type LGMs from 1955 onwards, but was cast into jail by a disbelieving authority when he tried to raise money to develop technologies based on the supersciences they had imparted to him. To George Van Tassell (1910–78) the LGMs – "Etherians" – revealed not just how to build a device that would cure ageing, sadly left incomplete at his death, but also the principles of interplanetary travel, summarized for us by W. Raymond Drake in *Gods or Spacemen*:

> the Etherians ionize a portion of etheric space, attune their thoughts to their destination, where their ship instantly arrives, decrease their vibratory frequency until their ship materializes into our Earth's atmosphere, while the reverse process of transcendence returns them at once to their own plane. This accounts for the fantastic appearances and disappearances so puzzling to terrestrial observers. The etheric ships one moment are on Venus and virtually the next moment manifest above Earth.

The human-like aliens met by George Adamski (1891–1965) and the circumstances under which he met them are too numerous to be within our scope here. For further details the interested reader is referred to *Flying Saucers Have Landed* by Desmond Leslie and Adamski himself.

**ABOVE Howard and Connie Menger.** Howard claimed that during the 1950s he was frequently visited by interstellar travellers.

**BELOW Reinhold Schmidt,** who suffered at the hands of the law when he tried to raise capital to finance the development of technologies imparted to him by the interstellar travellers whom he met often from 1955 onwards.

# THE MEN IN BLACK

A quite separate human-like entity involved with UFO encounters is the Man in Black – it seems curious to use the term in the singular, because they always operate in either pairs or trios. They have blandly unmemorable faces, dress in well-pressed black suits, wear black hats and sometimes black sunglasses (which if removed reveal glowing eyes), drive around in big black limos and, disguised as someone in the anonymous branch of officialdom (such as the secret services or the Internal Revenue), call on you to make threatening noises a couple of days after you have had an encounter with the occupants of a UFO; their territory is apparently restricted to the USA. One of their more irritating habits is that of stealing items of evidence that would have proved beyond doubt that your UFO encounter was genuine.

Most of the tales of MIBs seem to be born of paranoia; a few quite possibly are the product of overzealous government security agents checking up on things or of souvenir hunters pretending to be such in order to purloin UFO-related materials. The very first version of the MIB scenario came from one Albert K. Bender, who the year before had founded the grandiosely named International Flying Saucer Bureau, a one-man-and-a-dog organization sans dog. When he closed it down abruptly in 1953 he claimed to have done so because, although he had uncovered the ultimate solution to the whole flying-saucer mystery, he had been heavily leaned on by three MIBs not to divulge it . . . or else. Most of his associates uncharitably assumed that Bender had merely run out of money for and/or interest in the IFSB but that he hadn't liked to go with a whimper rather than a bang. Nevertheless, the MIB saga persisted. The three MIBs who visited Bender (in his later versions they were accompanied by women clad in skimpy white dresses) stank of sulphur and told him that they had come from a distant galaxy "dominated" by an immense burning mass beyond human conception". As soon as quasars, then thought to be curious very bright stars, first came into the public consciousness in 1963, the wider-eyed ufologists immediately began to look to them as sources of extraterrestrial visitors, and so it was hardly surprising that some later MIBs said that they came from the planet of just such a star, a matter confirmed by a number of other ufonauts. Of course, we now know that quasars are incredibly distant and highly energetic galaxies with extremely active nuclei. This is astonishingly like Bender's original description, but that may be no more than coincidence. Certainly it's curious that ufonauts got mixed up about the nature of quasars during exactly the same period that terrestrial scientists misunderstood the objects' nature.

ABOVE **A drawing by Al Bender of one of the Men in Black who had attempted to intimidate him into silence.**

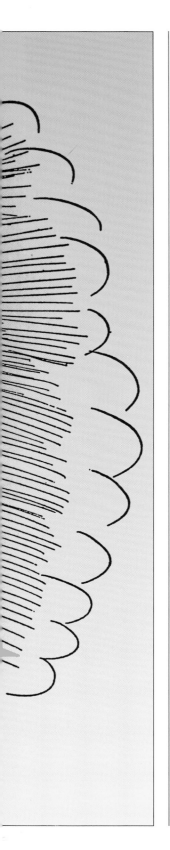

The link between Fairyland and the ufonauts will have been evident on a number of occasions during this discussion. At random we can note the Kelly-Hopkinsville "goblins", as they were and are widely known: the analogy goes beyond the mere naming, for these were smallish and, if not hostile, then certainly somewhat malicious-seeming creatures – although who wouldn't be if the introductory response from the visited was a gunshot? The tall and beautiful creatures, with their definite tang of erotism, could as well be elves from Fairyland as travellers from space. The monster of Flatwoods can be compared to an ogre or a ghost. The Men in Black (see page 72), with their bullying ways and their false assumption of the shield of authority, have their analogues in Fairyland. And the idea of the impossible mission, hinted at widely in the UFO literature, reminds one inevitably of tales like that of Rumpelstiltskin.

So the hypothesis that the Little People of Fairyland and the Little People from space are one and the same has a lot going for it, whether one wishes to regard the monsters concerned as physical ones or as psychological ones. In the latter event, we are drawn back to the notion that we touched on earlier: that each age and each culture creates its own selection of "other" beings, whose form is determined by the expectations of that age or culture. An extension of the concept is the proposal that the monsters are indeed there – that they have a genuine, objective existence beyond their equally genuine subjective existence – but that it is our perceptions of them that change according to our circumstances. In other words, whatever "real" form the monsters possess is so alien from our comprehension that we have to translate our perceptions of it into something acceptable to us.

# CHAPTER FOUR

# VAMPIRES AND WERE-WOLVES

## VAMPIRES

I t is hard to establish quite how many young women – virgin in appearance if not in fact – were murdered in the early 1600s at the behest of the Polish Countess Elizabeth de Báthory (d.1614), but the figure is generally regarded as lying somewhere between 300 and 650. Her motive for these murders was her desire to perpetuate her own beauty: she believed that bathing in the warm blood of the girls would

RIGHT **The early 17th-century Countess Elizabeth de Báthory, who believed she required the blood of young girls to retain her youthfulness.**

preserve her own youthful appearance. She and the servants who had followed her insane orders were finally brought to trial in 1611; that their crimes had been widely known among the peasantry of the surrounding countryside for some years before this, yet justice had failed to move against the aristocrat, shows us something of the workings of the 17th-century mind; as does the fact that the servants were burned alive for their crimes whereas their mistress was merely immured in her castle for the remaining few years of her life.

The Countess de Báthory's is an exceptional but, sadly, far from a unqiue case. There are other, surprisingly similar examples scattered throughout human history. The Roman Emperor Tiberius (42BC–AD37), having ruled with a fair degree of harsh distinction, spent the last 11 years of his life isolated on Capri, surrounded only by his servants. There he conducted a long orgy of self-gratification: alcohol, sex with women and children and, most repulsively, torture and execution for entertainment. The corpses of his victims, many of whom came to Capri assuming that the emperor's invitation to join him for some sport was

**BELOW** The castle of the de Báthory family where the countess and her servants committed their barbarous atrocities. Here she was immured for the rest of her days as punishment for her bestial crimes.

an honour, were cast over the nearby cliffs into the sea. Nothing was done to stop his crimes, even after they became well known, but the mob rejoiced in Rome on news of his death. Which was a bit premature of them: his successor was Caligula (AD12–41). The Roman Senate may have been slow to learn from the experience of being ruled by Tiberius and then Caligula, but learn they did: as Caligula's successor they chose the amiable near-idiot Claudius (10BC–AD54), on the basis that he would be too stupid to do anything other than what they told him to do. In fact, he was as sadistic as his predecessors, but had just enough animal cunning to remain within the bounds of what the Roman people were prepared to accept as natural law: he loved viewing the barbaric but of course perfectly legal execution of criminals, reintroducing some techniques of dispatch that even the Romans had abandoned as being inhumane.

Skipping forward about a millennium and a half, we come to the French Baron Gilles de Rais (or Retz; 1404–40), who fought heroically against the English alongside Joan of Arc, was marshal of France by the time he was 25, but then retired to his estates where, over the final decade of his life, he indulged in a sadistic orgy of mass rape-murder, his victims being at least 150 children. Unlike the Countess de Báthory, Tiberius and Claudius, he suffered the death penalty for his crimes.

The list of such empowered mass-murderers could be extended: Ezzelino da Romano (1184–1259), Tamerlane (1336–1405), Vlad the Impaler (d.1476), Ivan the Terrible (1530–84), Saddam Hussein (b.1937), Pol Pot (b.1928), Idi Amin (b.c.1925) . . . And, in a tragic demonstration of the will for democracy, modern serial sex-killers like Ted Bundy (1946–89) and the homosexual mass torture-murderer Dean Corll (1940–73) have, rather less publicly, perpetrated crimes equally vile, albeit on a necessarily smaller scale.

## EROTIC ORIGINS

There is a very genuine sense in which all of these people were vampires, in that all of them gloried in the shedding of other people's blood. More than that, they actually *required* it. There is no essential difference between a historical monster like Tiberius and a modern one like Pol Pot: the political system that they in large part helped to create permitted them and their cronies to perpetrate their crimes for extended periods, even though those crimes were public knowledge. We tend to forget that brutality is not the characteristic of regimes – or some similarly abstract political structure – but of collections of individual human beings, who in the cases cited have derived a very personal pleasure from the atrocities they have committed.

An artist's impression of Gilles de
Rais, military hero and sadistic mass murderer, watching in a state of
excitement as one of his servants prepares to despatch the next victim.
In the 1980s and early 1990s a campaign was mounted to rehabilitate
Gilles de Rais in the eyes of history, claiming that he himself was the
victim of a collossal frame-up on the part of jealous, local aristocrats

That pleasure is customarily, although perhaps not always, sexual in origin. The classic vampire of book, stage and screen is of course Dracula, created in 1897 by Bram Stoker (1847–1912) for his horror novel. The reason the book was so successful was almost certainly that Stoker, consciously or unconsciously, infused it with the eroticism commonly – indeed, almost always – associated with vampirism. Other, more recent

**RIGHT** **The Castle of Bran, in Transylvania, home of Vlad the Impaler, who inspired Bram Stoker's screen vampire, Dracula.**

fictions have been much more blatant about this. Anne Rice, in her "Vampire Chronicles" series of novels, takes great pains to make the link with eroticism as explicit as possible; while, rather earlier, Ron Goulart, in his "Vampirella" sries featuring the leggy, generously breasted, hip-swayingly, poutingly beautiful female vampire of that name, outrageously parodied the tradition. This sexual element seems certainly to be present in the cases of the historial vampires already mentioned: Elizabeth de Báthory, for example, although married, was certainly a lesbian, deriving erotic satisfaction as well as – she believed – youthfulness from her baths in the blood of her young female victims; and Gilles de Rais, a renowned homosexual (in an age where homosexuality might incur the death penalty), vastly preferred that his tragic little victims be boys, making do with girls only when there was no alternative.

The sexual correlation of vampirism, as it was regarded by our ancestors, was not necessarily purely erotic in origin: there was also a link between fecundity and the drinking of human blood. Annia Galeria Faustina, daughter of the Roman Emperor Antonius Pius (AD86–161) and wife of Marcus Aurelius (AD121–180), was so desperate to bear a son that she resorted to drinking the blood of unsuccessful gladiators. In this instance the vampirism seems to have been less involved with the enjoyment of pain and more with the widespread belief, common as late as the Middle Ages and still found today in some parts of the world, in the acquisition of virtues through cannibalism. Yet even cannibalism can be linked, exactly as with vampirism, with eroticism: the US mass-murderer Albert Fish (1870–1936), who brutally murdered perhaps 100 little girls (he was probably a homosexual, the repression of his instincts in an intolerant age leading to his sadomasochistic perversion), ate portions of at least some of his victims. The "Monster of Düsseldorf", Peter Kürten (1884–1931), murdered and raped at least nine children, cutting their throats and drinking their blood; in the letters he wrote from prison to the parents of some of his victims he said that drinking blood was to him as necessary a part of life as alcohol and cigarettes are for others. More recently, between 1979 and 1983, Dennis Nilsen (b.1945) murdered in his flat in north London up to 16 young homosexuals; his practice was to dissect the body, cook it and sometimes, although not always, eat parts of it. The truly horrifying thing about Nilsen's expression of the erotic/vampiric impulse is that this shy civil servant seemed to all who met him one of the gentlest and mildest of men. Albert Fish, too, had this modest demeanour: he was like everybody's favourite grandparent.

LEFT  The bathroom of the north London flat of the mass murderer Dennis Nilsen – site of some of the "processing" of his victims' bodies.

ABOVE **A famous illustration from a late 15th century German broadsheet showing Vlad enjoying his repast while watching his impaled victims in their death agonies.**

Vlad the Impaler – the Wallachian Prince Vlad IV – the acknowledged prototype for Stoker's Dracula, was rather more outgoing. In his day he was a military resistance leader and came to be regarded as something of a national hero because of his military campaigns. He derived his nickname from his habit of dealing with prisoners-of-war and anyone else who chanced to upset him, even trivially, by impaling them on poles: these were set vertically in the ground; the victim was lowered on to the sharp point and then left so that gravity and the victim's agonized writhings slowly drove the point up through the body. Vlad didn't take much upsetting: at least one of his officers was himself impaled for looking ill at the thought of dining while others were being impaled around him. Watching such spectacles – especially *en masse* – gave Vlad considerable pleasure: in effect, he fed on others' pain, requiring it as a sort of psychological nutrition. It can be speculated that the bites that sadistic sex killers very commonly inflict upon their victims are a physical expression of this psychological craving.

The vampires of fable – the classic vampires to which we shall turn shortly – are of course rather different. They are not murderers suffering from some poorly understood psychological ailment but supernatural beings. They are "living dead" who may venture abroad only by night, sleeping during the day because direct sunlight – as surely as a stake through the heart – spells their doom. They are shapeshifters (a common characteristic of folkloric bogeymen) – that is, they may alter their form from that of a human to that of a bat. Their victims, traditionally, may "survive" the bloodletting at the cost of themselves becoming vampires.

## CHARACTERIZATION

This general outline of the vampire is found throughout a surprisingly wide range of epochs and diversity of cultures. We can see in the composite characterization a number of basic elements of folk legends. Shapeshifting, as noted, is one: a modern version of the shapeshifter is the phantom hitch-hiker. Likewise, the concept of the living dead is found in many parts of the world – zombies are the most obvious exemplar – as can that of the creature who must shun daylight. In one or two vampire legends the monster is distinguished by having its feet "fitted on backwards". All these characteristics, as well as the vampire's need to drink blood from the living, can be placed in the category of "fundamental fears"; that is, they pluck at terrors that are buried deeply inside each one of us, whatever our cultural background. Even people from advanced technological cultures are affected by these fundamental fears: it is not at all surprising that they surface even in high-tech futuristic science fiction.

## FEMALE AGGRESSORS

Some vampire legends exert a further fascination in that the aggressors are females. Here the dominance is being exercised by the "wrong" sex, and the audacity of this "perversion" of the "natural order of things" is in itself erotic. The male is helpless in the vampiress's clutches and so

LEFT *Sixth Palace of Hell*, painting by Fay Pomerance depicting Lilith tempting a dying man with the voluptuousness of her flesh.

*cannot be held responsible for whatever acts then ensue.* (The same could be said of succubi, the female demons said to be responsible for men's erotic dreams, draining the sleeper of not only semen but also some poorly defined vital essence. Succubi have always been much more popular objects of dread than their male counterparts, incubi. Hebraic legends speak of the Lilith, a vampiric demon who to the early Christians was the Queen of the Succubi; in fact, the Lilith was a borrowing from the Babylonians. A different interpretation has Lilith as the evil female

ABOVE **Myra Hindley and Ian Brady, the infamous Moors Murderers, who torture-murdered several children, feeding on the "psychic energy" of their screaming victims.**

creature who was Adam's first wife; it is not surprising that some misogynistic scholars went one further, equating her with Eve.) It is no coincidence that an entire, successful subgenre of pornography is based – as are many "schoolteacher" prostitutes' incomes – on this dominatrix scenario: the man is freed from any feelings of guilt about what happens because he is powerless to counter the woman's, or preferably women's, nymphomania. The link between this "perverted" dominance and vampirism finds its clear fictional expression not only in parts of Stoker's *Dracula* but also, perhaps most overtly of all, in a number of the tales of C(atherine) L. Moore (b.1911). Of these Peter Nicholls has remarked in *The Encyclopedia of Science Fiction:*

> It might be expected that the image of woman as all-engulfing Holy Prostitute and She-Fiend would be an exclusively masculine fantasy, but – perhaps because it is at least an image of power in a world where, during the era of the pulp magazines, women were relatively powerless – it attracted some women writers. C. L. Moore made a speciality of such figures, notably in her Northwest Smith tales. The Medusa creature, "Shambleau", in Moore's 1933 story of that name is an archetype of the female as a fantasy of sexual horror: "From head to foot he was slimy from the embrace of the crawling horror about him . . . and the look of terrible ecstasy that overspread (his face) seemed to come from somewhere far within . . ."

Shambleau was a vampire in all but name, albeit one that was encountered far in the future and on a distant planet. The true horror – and the true erotism – has nothing to do with the "slime" or the "crawling": it is a product of the female exercising dominance.

## MOTIVATION

The necessity to dominate other human beings is customarily born from an individual's personal inadequacy: the motive is to gain reassurance through constant "proof" to oneself that one is not only not a second-rate human being but, contrastingly, a more powerful and vibrant personality than one's fellows. As in cases of rape, most of the historical vampires mentioned above were expressing their power over people who were utterly defenceless. The Countess de Báthory, Tiberius and Gilles de Rais had armies of servants to ensure that their unhappy victims had no chance of escape. Ian Brady (b.1938) and Myra Hindley (b.1942), who used a tape-recorder to preserve the "psychic energy" they desired from their victims.

PROCES CRIMINEL
DE MESSIRE GILLES
DE BRETAGNE BARON DE
RAIZ MARECHAL DE FRANCE
LEQVEL·FVT·EXECVTÉ·LE·
20 OCTOBRE · 1440

*The execution of Gilles de Rais, the 15th-century vampire responsible for the torture-murders of about 150 children.*

It is easy enough to believe that the people capable of such evils must be inspired not by any human impulse but by "something else" – an evil spirit, perhaps – that has invaded them, has possessed their mind. Such an explanation has been frequently proffered in cases of vampiric murder, but it is facile: it is an attempt to fob off on to the supernatural the responsibility for actions that were committed by human beings who were in possession of human minds. It is unpleasant to have to admit that a human mind can become so twisted as to contemplate such deeds: much easier to blame it all on evil spirits. Yet clearly vampirism is a psychological condition – albeit one of which we have yet only a poor understanding. Whether it is social or genetic in origin, or a mixture of both, is something that we do not as yet know – although we can note that many vampires have suffered from, an "over-parented" childhood: either they have been treated with excessive strictness or they have been subjected to a surfeit of pampering. However, this is certainly not the whole explanation: far more girls than boys have tormented childhoods through sexual abuse, and yet far fewer women than men are guilty of vampiric crimes.

## CLASSIC VAMPIRES

Fears of the traditional vampire still survive in many parts of the world, and are far from extinct in the West. In 1973 a Polish expatriate, Demetrius Myiciura, was found dead in his flat in Stoke-on-Trent, UK. He had choked to death on a clove of garlic which he had obviously been in the habit of putting in his mouth last thing at night; on his windowsill was a bowl of urine into which garlic had been mixed; salt had been sprinkled over his bed. Clearly Myiciura had been terrified of nocturnal vampiric attack, and his death had come about solely because of his belief. Belief by the perpetrator in the powers to be gained through vampirism – literal, blood-sucking vampirism – has been responsible for other deaths in comparatively recent times. One such individual, a man called Sal-varrey, was arrested in 1910 near Galazanna, Portugal, after the body of a child, drained of blood, had been discovered: he confessed to the murder, declaring it to be an inevitable result of the fact that he was a vampire and required blood. The English killer John Haigh (1910–49), the Acid Bath Murderer, was another. He had a typical vampire's childhood: his parents were Plymouth Brethren who depirved the boy of virtually all of the luxuries of modern life, up to and including friendships with others of his own age, and instilled in him a belief in the literal truth of the Bible, including the parts about washing in the blood of the Lamb. He killed nine people, dissolving their bodies in acid, but not before drinking of their blood. Although the court refused to accept his plea of vampirism (which the defence maintained was a form of insanity), it seems likely that it was genuine.

Haigh had no interest in the "psychic nutrition" we have talked about – indeed, as a good Christian, he inflicted as little pain as possible on his victims, dispatching them with rapid efficiency: instead, his objective was their blood, the drinking of which he required for his own spiritual advancement.

This is very close indeed to the classic vampire; and Haigh was not alone. In the mid-1960s an Argentinian called Florencia Roque Fernandez confessed to the police that he had preyed on women at night, biting at their throats. He didn't know what drove him to do this. In 1913, in London, a woman called "Scotch Dolly" was found beaten to death; among her injuries were nearly 40 little double wounds along one of her legs. Her killer was never discovered, but the nature of those wounds is certainly suggestive. In 1874, in Rhode Island, a man was arrested for digging up the corpse of his daughter and burning her heart; this was, he claimed, the only way he could stop her from draining the lifeblood of the other members of the family.

## THE LIVING DEAD

Here is another aspect of the vampire: the ability to arise from the dead unless well and truly stopped by some means such as staking through the heart. This belief is very much akin to that concerning the zombies of Haiti: these undead can be raised from their graves by sorcerers just so long as the deed is done before the body has had time to rot, and

BELOW **This stylized painting by Camy Rocher depicts a voodoo ritual in progress. The attendants and sorcerer are preparing to sacrfice a goat in order to invoke a tree spirit.**

dutiful relatives therefore heap graves with boulders and stand guard to preclude sorcerous attentions until decay has done its work. (The Haitian penal code has a clause declaring that among the definitions of poisoning is the use of drugs to reduce someone to "a state of lethargy", and it is likely that is is such a practice that has given fuel to the zombie legend.) Similar precautions were taken in ancient Greece – especially on the island of Thera, where the problem was particularly acute – to protect the newly dead from the depredations of the *vrukalakos*, a creature who could restore the corpses to life: the undead then preyed upon the living. The hallmarks of the *vrukalakos* were red hair, blue eyes and birthmarks, so a deal of innocent suspects, as ever, lost their lives. Other ghoulish creatures to avoid included the *striges*, who (reports differed) could be either blood-sucking birds that snatched babes from the cradle or exquisite humaniform vampires; and revenants, who were actually goodies, of virility sufficient that they could fight off death in order to carry on fighting baddies, but who required regular doses of human blood in order to keep their strength up.

Also from ancient Greece (and surviving into Roman times) there was the *lamia*, or *empusa*, a beautiful vampiric seductress whose embraces debilitated a man much as did those of the succubus; they would wait until the man reached an ecstatic climax before going for the throat (which description, yet again, would seem to tell us a lot about male sexual hang-ups). Philostratus (*c*.170–245) described one of these in his *Life of Apollonius of Tyana*.

**ABOVE  Title-page of the *Dispensarium* of "Nicolai Propositus". The fish-tailed figure on the left is of the *lamia*, a vampiric, demonic seductress.**

## THE RISEN UNDEAD

*In ancient India a vampire was raised to the deity in the form of the goddess Kali. At less elevated levels were the vile, cannibalistic Rékshasas, who were once more the risen undead. The ancient Babylonians and Assyrians had the ekimmu, which was a vampiric restless spirit, the soul of someone who had during life violated any of the myriad religious taboos that structured society – including even the mode of death, for virtually any way of dying except of old age in one's bed was taboo. There were a lot of the ekimmu about. In The Vampire: His Kith and Kin Montague Summers (not always the most reliable of authorities), notes that belief in the risen undead and their vampiric requirements seems to be worldwide and transcendent of time.*

If the belief in the ability of the dead to rise – and this is a quite different matter from the reappearances of the dead as ghosts – is so universal, can there be any explanation for it? Rather depressingly, there can. One of the ways in which vampires could be, as it were, diagnosed was that, when their graves were dug up to check, the body would be found to be unaffected by the natural processes of decay – indeed, hair and nails would have grown and the complexion would be if anything ruddier than in life. The likely conclusion that we can draw is that the converse was the case: *the body was displaying many of the symptoms of death while being in fact alive.* In an age when medicine was still somewhat rudimentary, the likelihood of a coma being identified as such was, to say the least, minimal. Much more probable is that the unfortunate sufferer was assumed to have died and was therefore buried while still alive. We know from countless examples that such accidental premature burials did take place, because there are pathetic evidences such as clawing marks on the inside of coffins where the unfortunates, wakening, desperately tried to free themselves from their hideous prison; how much more frequently must comatose victims never have recovered consciousness, remaining apparently dead in their coffins until the real thing finally snuffed them out, the only signs that they had survived far longer than believed being such features as the growth of hair and nails?

In a curious way, then, those frightened men who dug up graves and found the occupants "supernaturally" well preserved, and who then decapitated the corpse or burnt it or drove a stake through its heart, were probably doing at least some of the comatose a considerable favour; for they were precluding the possibility of the person later wakening to find himself or herself interred.

As we have seen, we can explain most of the vampire phenomenon in reasonably mundane terms, ranging from psychology through sheer human credulity to premature burial. We are still left with a few unsettling questions, but this is only to be expected in an area that has been so little subjected to any formal scientific analysis. How does the casebook look for the apparently related monster, the werewolf?

# WEREWOLVES

### LYCANTHROPY

Before we take a look at it, we should be aware that the word "lycanthropy" is generally taken to have two quite distinct meanings, although the two are related. A werewolf – that is, someone who quite literally turns into a wolf or wolf-like creature, and back again – may be termed a lycanthrope (as may be, by extension, a person who can transform into any other animal); but the word can be applied also to

**BELOW  A werewolf fleeing with the child it has snatched; a drawing by the 15th/16th-century German artist Lucas Cranach.**

A ce Monstre attaqua une femme avec ses trois enfans
en emporta un agé de 18 ans, cette tendre mere animé
du courage maternelle se jeta sur ce monstre qui
la porta un quart d'heure sur son dos elle fut
heureusement delivré elle et ses enfans par l'arrivée
d'un homme et de son chien, elle fut recompensé
par sa Majesté

B Cette Bete cruelle devora
le 22 Avril dernier un enfant
de 12 a 18 ans près le Village
de Prunières 1764

Ce monstre le 12 Janvier
5 enfans qui gardoient leur
prit un par la tête et le
se mirent à la poursuivre
geusement qu'il firent tach
et sauverent leur compagn
donner une recompense

those who suffer from a rare (but not exceptionally rare) mental illness which causes them to *believe* that they have undergone the transformation. As we shall see, the distinction may well be a false one. Werewolves share with vampires many of the classic characteristics of folkloric monsters. They, too, are capable of shapeshifting, obviously, and equally obviously they use their supernaturally augmented strength to overpower and devour their victims. The similarity of characteristics is far from merely a coincidence: it would seem likely that, early on, popular conceptions about vampires were grafted on to the dread felt towards wolves, a dread that was very real, and far from foolish, among the peasantry of medieval Europe. Certainly the two varieties of monster were bound together in close association in numerous different beliefs as to their natural history. According to one school of thought, werewolves, on death, became vampires. According to another, vampires and werewolves were distinct creatures but the two species practised a sort of social symbiosis: werewolves, in this scheme, were not shapeshifters but wolf-like creatures with some human characteristics; vampires, on the other hand, could alter their appearance so as to live undetected among human societies, their contribution to the bloodthirsty partnership being to befriend isolated humans and lure them off to solitude in the forest, where both species could indulge in feasting.

**ABOVE** This engraving shows the children of Gévaudan gallantly fighting off the beast when it attacked them.

89

Returning to the classic model of the werewolf – the shapeshifter who was "human" for most of the time – another belief concerning lycanthropes was that, when in their human guise, they had a layer of subcutaneous hair; thus, when the time came to transform themselves into wolves, they simply, as it were, turned their skins inside-out. This belief led to the barbaric slaughter of countless innocent suspects, caught in the same sort of Catch-22 as those who underwent ducking on suspicion of witchcraft; but drowning must have been better than being flayed alive. In the Slavic countries babies born with cauls over their heads were believed to be werewolves and thereby contributed to the already high infant mortality rates.

It seems – certainly at a first glance – unlikely that the shapeshifting werewolf of the classic model has ever existed. It may be that the notion was, as we saw, nothing more than an exaggeration of the dread towards the vicious wolves of the forests. But it is possible that the other version of the legend we noted has more than a grain of truth in it. It is not at all beyond the bounds of feasibility that the forests were also the home of a large, wolf-like carnivore whose frequent prey consisted of human beings who for some reason allowed themselves to be cut down out of sight of their fellows. If we ignore people who chose to lead eremitic existences – and whose disappearances would anyway almost certainly go unnoticed – there were still ample opportunities for our hypothetical carnivore to strike. In our own densely populated society, where more effort must be put into preserving nature than into taming it, we tend to forget that a few hundred years ago the situation was very much the reverse. Centres of population were extremely small by our standards – medieval York, for example, was lucky if it had the population of what we would today regard as a decent-sized village – and they were far between. The true unit of population was the hamlet, with isolated homes scattered around it and often enough separated from it by tracts of virtually virgin forest. Thus there must have been many a Little Red Riding Hood who, in order to take food to her aged grandmother, had to go through the deep, dark forest; and many, too, who never returned from that expedition. Natural hazards and genuinely human monsters must certainly have taken their toll of such individuals, so giving rise to legends such as that of the werewolf; but there is nothing to dictate that those legends were not without some reasonable foundation in reality.

Why, then, are there no traces today of this hypothetical carnivore? An immediate response is that, if the beast was much like the wolf (except, perhaps, more intelligent, and also tailless – an occasionally mentioned characteristic of werewolves), then the ecological circum-

stance was untenable. As evolution has taught us over and over again, ecologies are not stable when two different species are vying for the same niche within them. (By "niche" we are talking about what one might regard as a role. An ecology is stable when all the roles within it are filled. The large predators can be regarded as the leading players, ensuring that the soubrettes – the smaller carnivores and the herbivores – don't soon come to dominate the production. But the vast cast of extras – the vegetation – is just as necessary if the performance as a whole is to succeed.) This is especially true if the niche is such a pivotal one as that occupied by the largest predator within an ecology such as a forest; and especially so if the ecology itself is under attack from outside, as the medieval forests were to be over the succeeding centuries. In the end the onslaught of humankind was to be too great for even the wolf itself to survive in most parts of Europe; but, during the process of the wolf's extinction, it and its hypothetical rival must have fought like the wild creatures they were for occupation of the ecological niche both claimed. And, despite the greater intelligence of our werewolves, they were inevitably destined to be the losers in this contest: they lacked the pack instinct and hence the ability to organize themselves in sufficient numbers to present any form of coordinated resistance.

ABOVE **A 16th-century German illustration showing a werewolf setting about its victim in full public view.**

Or so we may speculate. Another hypothesis is that, being so intelligent, the wererwolves simply became more secretive, hiding themselves away cunningly from the depredations of *Homo sapiens*, maintaining family-sized groups in remote parts of the countryside or even in the urban jungle and still preying on society's outcasts. The proposition is supported by a strange case that occurred in Le Gevaudan, south-central France, in the 1760s. Over a period of three years the villagers of the surrounding area were subject to wild attacks by an apparently wolf-like creature that seemed to display an uncanny cunning. In 1765, 1766 and 1767 Louis XV rather desultorily sent military expeditions in an attempt to exterminate the creature that was slaughtering his villagers; the third of these was successful, and the corpse was paraded around the region to reassure everyone that the terror was over. There are no proper accounts of the corpse's appearance, but off-hand mention was made of its feet, which were more like hoofs than like a wolf's paws.

**RIGHT King Louis XV of France feared that the peasants' terror might flare into open revolt, and ordered the Royal Hunt Master to kill the beast.**

## THE PHANTOM HITCH-HIKER

*It is tempting to link the werewolf-as-failed-wolf-competitor with the numerous reports there have been of phantom hitch-hikers.*

*The phantom hitch-hiker has entered the annals of what is described as urban legend, one of those incredible tales that are passed around, usually orally but rather too often via down-market newspapers and television programmes, and that are regarded by both teller and audience as being factual, no matter how impossible they in fact are. Excellent collections of them have been compiled by, among others, Rodney Dale and, more especially, Jan Harold Brunvand. A typical urban legend concerning a phantom hitch-hiker would run approximately as follows. A young person, male (less commonly female), is driving home alone at night. He spots a hitch-hiker and picks him (rarely her) up. There is something definitely peculiar about the passenger: ideally, the driver suddenly notices that one hitherto-hidden hand of the passenger is hairy and clawed. Somewhere during the journey, the driver gets rid of the stranger, either by evicting him (usually by subterfuge) or through the passenger simply melting out of existence. At journey's end, there is nothing to show that the encounter ever took place . . . except, perhaps, a single hairy paw, severed at the wrist . . .*

*Michael Goss, who has written what is probably the most rigorous examination of the phantom hitch-hiker from the viewpoint of the non-urban-folklorist,* The Evidence for Phantom Hitch-Hikers, *concludes that there is indeed an underlying reality, but that it is a subjective one. "One reason the Phantom Hitch-hiker retains its glamour," he remarks, "is that the ghost is still useful to us. The motif is not an archaic closed system, but a form adaptable to the needs of the hour." One can accept this point while at the same time regarding the phantom hitch-hiker not as a ghost tailored to the modern world but as a memory, corrupted in order to accord with our technological state, of infernally clever but nevertheless quite solidly corporeal creatures who bedevilled solitary travellers in times past and – who knows? – may still do so: we hear the stories of the drivers who reach their destination, but what of the others?*

### THE WOLF SPIRIT

Although in fiction there are various accounts of people deliberately setting out to become vampires – the advantages of the state include immortality – there seem to be no such instances in fact. The same is not true of the werewolf state; presumably it must have seemed to the vengeful like quite a good idea to be able to rip their foes apart with ease and, if fortune smiled and their condition went unsuspected, with impunity. What was required was that the individual called upon the

BELOW Relations between real wolves and humans have sometimes been friendlier than we might expect from werewolf tales and even from the history books. Romulus and Remus, the legendary founders of Rome, having been abandoned as babies, were suckled through infancy by a she-wolf.

"Wolf Spirit" through the use of complicated rituals and the liberal application of such ingredients as opium and the fat from a freshly slaughtered cat. (The opium would suggest that the transformation was, in reality, a psychological rather than a physical one.) Once the "Wolf Spirit" had agreed to the supplicant's request for a contract, the individual would ever thereafter have human form during the hours of daylight and wolfish form between sunset and dawn. Werewolves could be wounded or killed just as could normal wolves (the requirement for a silver bullet through the heart, or for a bullet that had been blessed in a chapel dedicated to St Hubert, was a later sophistication), but in either event they would revert to their human condition. On death the werewolf might become a vampire, and so its body should be cremated – a wise precaution, anyway.

One source of werewolf legends must certainly be the examples there have occasionally been, throughout history, of children being fostered in the wild by animals: the legend of Romulus and Remus was not spun out of merely imaginary threads. The wolf – that vicious, merciless predator – might seem an unlikely candidate for such philanthropy, being more likely to dine on than to succour an abandoned child, yet in fact wolves have a vile reputation not wholly supported by the facts: certainly they are the most frequently mentioned of all animals in such accounts. In this century the instances have largely been not in Europe but in the Indian subcontinent. In 1920, for example, a missionary to Midnapore, the Reverend F. Singh, succeeded in "rescuing" two little girls from their life as adopted wolfcubs, a life to which they seem to have adapted completely and happily. Which is more than could be said of their return to human society: the younger, about 18 months old when found, died within the year, and the older, perhaps eight at the time of capture, survived only a further nine years. Similar tales were widely reported in Europe when wolves were more plentiful there: they were obviously regarded as fascinating rarities rather than as bizarre violations of the natural order and thus evil abominations.

In this early illustration of a
werewolf savaging a young woman the erotic connotations evident in the
whole corpus of legends about vampires and werewolves is especially
emphasized.

## THE WEREWOLF MYTHOS

Not so the werewolf. Theories as to their nature varied, but many, if they declined to accept the possibility of a complete physical transformation, involved evil spirits: these were either truly supernatural, possessing the bodies of wolves and humans alternately; or were the vile spirits of corrupted humans, who were capable of taking on a wolf's form while leaving their human body safely stashed elsewhere. This latter hypothesis was maintained by the 15th century Pierre Mamor, Rector at the University of Poitiers, even though one of his less charming

**LEFT One possible theory of the werewolf myth is the practice of warriors donning the skins of wild animals. Other theories involve the supernatural.**

anecdotes concerned a peasant, in human form, throwing up the hand and arm of a child, devoured while he was in his wolfish form. The literature is full of 15th century and later instances of apprehended cannibalistic mass child-murderers confessing to having committed their crimes in the form of wolves, but it is hard to take them seriously; the methods used to extract confessions in those times were such that the unfortunate suspects were willing to admit to virtually anything that the lurid imaginations of their inquisitors might spawn. Yet other anecdotes have a certain naïve charm. Olaus Magnus (or Magni; 1490–1558) recounts in his *Historia de Gentibus Septentrionalibus* (1555), possibly written in part by his elder brother Johannes, Archbishop of Uppsala, one such tale. A Russian gentlewoman was one day pontificating on the impossibility of there being any such creature as the werewolf when one of her servants shyly interrupted her. The transformation was possible, he affirmed, and by way of proof he swiftly turned himself into a wolf before the eyes of herself and her guests. Unfortunately, the dogs went for the seeming wolf, inflicting terrible injuries on it – including gouging out its eye – before it could escape. When the "human" servant reappeared a few days later, he was indeed missing an eye. The tale is, of course, more implausible than most of its ilk: would servant or mistress be so blasè about the whole thing, and, anyway, surely the gouging out of an eye was a most improbable injury for a dog to be able to wreak. A similar and oft-cited story comes from the Auvergne. A hunter encountered an aristocrat in the forest and was invited to bring back his spoils, after the hunt, to the aristocrat's château for a bit of feasting. Later in the day the hunter was attacked by a vicious wolf. In driving it off he amputated its paw, which he kept as a souvenir. On nearing the château he found to his astonishment that it had turned into a woman's hand; and, when he arrived at his host's home, it was soon discovered that the ring on one of the hand's fingers belonged to the aristocrat's wife. Of course, her ladyship was then located, clutching the stump of her wrist; confessing her guilt, she was sent to the stake. This latter anecdote is far too well constructed a tale for any credence at all to be given to it.

We note that in Olaus Magnus' anecdote there was no question of the werewolf being malignant, and there are a surprising number of tales about kindly, benevolent werewolves. This may have been because, as we have noted, in real life wolves are not necessarily always vicious creatures, despite their reputation. A person who had survived an encounter with a real wolf might well believe that its behaviour was so "out of character" that it must be possessed of some kind of human gentility.

Another possible root of the werewolf mythos might have been the practice of warriors of donning the skins of wild animals. The practice was probably born from the idea that an animal skin attested to the courage and/or strength of the warrior, in that he had succeeded in killing the wild animal concerned; the next step was that the ferocity of the animal was imparted to the man; if the warrior himself believed this

ABOVE **A medieval print of a monstrous wolf attacking a man having undergone lycanthropy (shape-changing).**

to be the case, then indeed he would conjure himself into such a mental state that, like a berserker (literally a warrior clothed in bearskin), he would seem to have the strength of ten and fight with mindless ferocity until the last vestiges of life left him. Moreover, like the man in the embrace of the succubus, he would in no ways be responsible for the actions he performed while in his animalistic guise – a good thing, since the barbarities perpetrated by such warriors were often of a gratuitous cruelty that no wild animal would have had the imagination, let alone the will, to emulate. To any lucky enough to survive the attacks of such butchers, it might have seemed inconceivable that they were human, even though in many ways they *looked* somewhat human. In *Man into Wolf* Robert Eisler has suggested that such confusion might have been created more definitively, in that the migratory seasons of wolf-packs corresponded approximately to those of the predatory berserkers, so that there was little to choose between the furry animals that attacked your village one day and the fur-clad monsters that attacked it the next; this hypothesis seems to me to be a lily-gilder. Conversely, when not in "warrior mode", such men might indeed be capable of kindliness and charity – hence the confusing accounts of benevolent ·verewolves. Hence, too, the accounts of wolfmen in Ireland being respected members of courtly retinues; according to Nennius, these "Ossory wolves" retransformed themselves into wolves only when they bit – which sounds like an exact description, in metaphor, of the berserker phenomenon.

And yet another source might be truly ancient legends such as that of the Greek Lycaeon, King of Arcadia and father of the nymph Calisto. There are various versions of the tale. One has Lycaeon foolishly sacrificing a child in order to ingratiate himself with Zeus (a story that sounds familiar); another, recounted by Ovid, says that Lycaeon, eager to test whether or not Zeus really was omniscient, served him with human flesh in place of meat to see if the god would spot the difference. Either way, Zeus was displeased and converted Lycaeon into a wolf as punishment (and a pretty mild punishment, bearing in mind Zeus's habit of transforming his ex-seducees into wild creatures – Calisto, Lycaeon's daughter, for example, was turned into a bear). Then there were the Maenads, who often donned wolf-masks for their orgies, at the climax of which they would pursue and rip to pieces an animal or, sometimes, a human being. And, from Norse mythology, we have the Fenris wolf, born to the god Loki (himself partial to occasional appearances in wolfish form) and the giantess Angrboda. Fenris had a lousy childhood – hidden away by his father, who was ashamed of him because the marriage to Angrboda had not been authorized by the other gods, then brought to Asgard by Odin, who attempted to educate him into more civilized

ABOVE 10th-century Viking slab showing Odin attacked by the Fenris wolf.

LEFT Great bronze of Zeus, who was believed to have transformed his ex-seducees into wild creatures.

ways. It is hardly surprising that Fenris became resentful; and tales of his resentfulness might have been transmuted into the blanket hostility that the werewolf, in many legends, displays towards human beings.

It might be thought that the werewolf – *pace* the phantom hitch-hiker – was a creature lost to us some centuries ago, but there are some reports that are much more recent. They are irritatingly anecdotal in nature – as are most reports, when examined at any level beyond the cursory, in the field of cryptozoology – but the very fact that they have been widely accepted would indicate that, in at least one sense, the werewolf is still with us.

One story was apparently told by a French farmer who died in 1927. One day about the turn of the century he was out walking on his land when he spotted two wolves coming towards him. Rather than argue the issue, he shot up a tree. The wolves paused beneath his hiding-place and conversed for a while in comprehensible French; *en passant* one of them lifted his tail, produced a snuffbox and proffered it to the other. Startled for some reason, they suddenly fled, leaving the snuffbox behind them. The farmer was able to identify it and return it to its owner. He had recognized the two werewolves but refused to divulge their names until, many years later, one of them died. The "man's" grave was soon found to be nightly subjected to scrabblings on the part of clawed paws . . .

Another refers to 1960 when a certain Harold Young was hunting in the Thailand/Burma border country. He arrived at night at one village and was met by terrified villagers who told him that there was a taw (jungle werewolf) at work there. Hearing a scream, Young and his men rushed to find the body of a woman, her neck still being gnawed by the taw. Young shot the beast, but the visibility was poor – there was only the moonlight – and all he succeeded in doing was wounding it. The next day Young and his men followed the trail of blood that the injured creature had left behind it in its flight; this trail led off into the jungle for a while, but then turned and came back into the village, finishing up outside one hut in particular. Inside the hut they found a man with a bullet-wound in his side.

Once again, both tales seem a little too good to be true. But whether they are complete fabrications or hugely embellished versions of events that did actually take place is something that we shall probably never know.

**ABOVE Engraving by George Jacob Schneider of a werewolf that is supposed to have terrified the region of Eschenbach, Germany, during the 1680s.**

## BATS AND VAMPIRES

*It would be wrong to close this discussion without briefly mentioning the relationship between bats and vampires, a relationship much emphasized in fiction, both printed and screened. In fact, the connection is a comparatively recent one, being made only once European settlers and zoologists had probed sufficiently far into Central and South America to discover the three species of vampire bats that dwell there. None of the species makes a habit of going for the throat and making two neat puncture-marks there; rather, they sneak up to the extremities of sleeping or even waking mammals, including humans, and make a tiny incision in the skin; they do not suck the blood, but lap it up with their nimble tongues as it emerges from the incision. All three species are very small: the only animals to be in any danger of suffering debility through loss of blood from their attentions would have to be the object of repeated attack by a plurality of individuals. This is not to say that the tapped animals are at no risk from the vampires: like other species, these three are frequent bearers of rabies and other diseases.*

# CHAPTER FIVE

# MONSTERS OF THE DEEP

RIGHT **A lithograph after a bas relief formerly at Ninevah depicting Oannes, the Babylonian creature from the seas who taught mankind the rudiments of technology.**

In the first year there made its appearance, from a part of the Persian Gulf which bordered upon Babylonia, an animal endowed with reason who was called Oannes. The whole body of the animal was like that of a fish; and had under a fish's head another head, and also feet below, similar to those of a man, subjoined to the fish's tail. His voice, too, and language were articulate and human; and a representation of him is preserved even to this day.

This being in the daytime used used to converse with men; but took no food at that season; and he gave them an insight into letters and sciences and every kind of art. He taught them to construct houses, to found temples and to compile laws, and explained to them the principles of geometrical knowledge. He made them distinguish the seeds of the earth, and showed them how to collect fruits. In short, he instructed them in everything that could tend to soften manners and humanize mankind. From that time, so universal were his instructions, nothing material has been added by way of improvement. When the Sun set it was the custom of this being to plunge again into the sea, and abide all night in the deep; for he was amphibious.

After this there appeared other animals like Oannes . . .

Every culture has its own Creation myths, and it is perhaps unwise to take them too seriously, but the one from which the above extract is quoted deserves more careful consideration than most. First, it is concerned not with the origin of the world but, very particularly, with the origin of civilization; and, second, the civilization concerned was that of the Sumerians, and thus the ancestor of all extant human civilization. Our knowledge of the curious sea-beast Oannes and of his various successors, collectively called the Apkallu, is derived from the account given by a priest called Berosus, who lived around the time of Alexander the Great (356–323BC), long after the events described, which occurred at some time during or just before the 4th millennium BC. (The extract above is from a reporting of Berosus's work by Alexander Polyhistor. Two other versions exist, one by Abydenus and one by Apollodorus.)

It is a sobering thought that a monster from the deep may have given our species the gift of civilization, providing the foundations for our arts, sciences, mathematics and – most important of all at the time – agriculture. These are gifts more normally associated with god (or the gods), yet there is no suggestion in any of the versions of Berosus that the Apkallu were regarded as deities: they were "personages" or "strange beings". Much has been made – notably by Carl Sagan in *Intelligent Life in the Universe* with I. S. Shklovskii) and by Robert K. G. Temple in *The Sirius Mystery* – of the possibility that the Apkallu were beings from an extraterrestrial civilization who instructed our ancestors in the basic sciences, thus giving our species a leg-up towards what has become a flourishing technological civilization. It can reasonably be speculated, on the basis of the descriptions given of Oannes and the rare surviving pictorial representations of him/it (all of which date from long after, of course), that he/it was approximately humanoid but not an air-breather, the fish's head and body described being in fact an airtight suit complete with helmet, like a modern spacesuit. The alien mission, according to the speculation, passed on elementary information to the "primitives" – including a warning of the Flood – for purposes at which we cannot sensibly guess, for to do so would be to make assumptions about alien psychology: it would be nice to think that the motives were of human type, being either philanthropic or based on loneliness (a very advanced species might wish to groom up another until a sharing of minds was possible). In fact, there are some flaws in any argument that the Apkallu were any more than a myth; however, there are similarly flaws in all attempts to discard them as purely a myth. And certainly human civilization did start rather abruptly, springing up from among predecessors that were, so far as can be established, substantially more primitive, as if some superbeing had indeed given human-kind a rapid injection of knowledge (although a prehistoric Archimedes might have had a similar effect).

# THE LOCH NESS MONSTER

We may never know the truth about the Apkallu unless, of course, one day we encounter their descendants among the wilderness of stars. Coming closer to home, there are other monsters assumed to live in the waters of our own world that certainly do not come from outer space but might as well do, so far are we from full knowledge of the mysteries of the ocean. Or even, it would seem, the mysteries of smaller bodies of water, namely lakes and rivers.

During 1987 an expedition searching Loch Ness, in Scotland, picked up sonar traces of an object which the expedition members believed to be a large fish or marine mammal; it was about the size of a large shark. The researchers dismissed suggestions that it might have been simply a

LEFT A startingly clear – *too* startlingly clear, say sceptics – photograph of the Loch Ness Monster taken in 1977 by Anthony "Doc" Shiels.

rock, on the very good grounds that, when they passed over the same area again later, the object was no longer there. They believed that they had finally come up with good evidence favouring the existence of the Loch Ness Monster – the classic case of all the world's lake and river monsters – although of course they had no means of telling what sort of animal the Loch Ness Monster might be. Further results were awaited with eagerness . . . and still are, five years later. With minor changes in detail, the same tale could be repeated about all of the monsters reputed to dwell in the lakes of the world.

There are a number of problems surrounding any claim that a huge creature dwells in the dark, cold waters of Loch Ness. The obvious one is that there cannot be just a single monster: there must be a whole extended family of them, because otherwise even an exceptionally long-lived creature would have died. But, if there are, say, a score or more monsters lurking there, why are sightings so rare? Another difficulty is that various observations of the creature(s) have differed quite dramatically from each other in their details, far more than could be expected among individuals of a single species: surely the loch cannot be inhabited by an *abundance* of unknown species!

One popular theory is that the Loch Ness Monster may be a surviving plesiosaur – the plesiosaur was a marine reptile whose heyday was the Age of the Dinosaurs, which ended about 65 million years ago for reasons that are themselves as yet not fully understood (probably the impact of a large meteorite or small cometary nucleus). The 1987 report might have seemed to support this hypothesis, because plesiosaurs looked very much like dolphins or sharks. Yet there are difficulties with this hypothesis, too. For one thing, for a long period before about 10,000 years ago Loch Ness was capped by a vast glacier. It would have been hard for any animal to have survived in the icy subglacial waters, if indeed there were any: Loch Ness may have been a solid block of ice. However, this objection assumes that the monster is not a comparatively recent immigrant: it is perfectly possible that a family of large marine creatures found its way into Loch Ness a mere few decades or centuries ago and have dwelled and bred there ever since. But again we come up against questions. These beasts could not be dolphins or whales, because for obvious reasons sightings would be commonplace; the same is true, although to a lesser extent, if we posit sharks. A far better bet might be giant squids, which would not only be reasonably secretive but also because partial observations of their complicated forms might account for the discrepancies among the many descriptions.

## EVIDENCE

Photographs of the Loch Ness Monster abound, but few prove convincing on analysis. Some are definite fakes; some are not quite that, but are certainly not pictures of anything very monstrous. The most famous of all the photographs purportedly of the creature, taken in 1934 by a visiting London surgeon, R. K. Wilson, seems convincing at first until one begins to make sensible estimates of the scale of the ripples surrounding the "monster's head"; conventional naturalists have proposed that the subject of the photograph was probably a diving otter or marine bird, perhaps a moorhen. Other photographs have been shown to be of floating logs. And others?

A stretch of movie film shot at the loch by Tim Dinsdale on 23 April 1960 shows what seems to be a hump moving slowly away from the camera and then, perhaps on being alerted to Dinsdale's presence, accelerating across the field of vision as it vanishes beneath the water. No rigorous explanation has yet been produced for this sighting; analysts of the film have tentatively concluded that the object was alive and, more definitely, that the maximum speed of the object was about 15kph (10omph) – about that of a steady human run – and that the "hump" was about 1.7m (5ft 6in) across. Several years later, on 13 June

The most famous of all the
photographs seeming to show the Loch Ness Monster, taken in 1934 by
the London surgeon R. K. Wilson. Orthodox naturalists are divided as
to what the picture might show.

1967, Richard Raynor took a film of a fast-moving wake with what appeared to be a living creature occasionally visible at its head. Raynor himself thought that the animal responsible might have been an otter, but analysis of the film shows that the exposed part of the animal alone was perhaps 2m (6ft 6in) long: some otter. In 1972–3 and again in 1975 underwater photography was used in the loch by a team headed by Dr Robert Rines. The results can only be described as inconclusive, for, even on the tiny minority of photographs which show anything other than the expected, the images are far from clear. One shows what can be interpreted as a plesiosaur-like flipper; another what can (with a stretch of the imagination) be construed to be a monstrous horned head, rather reminiscent of that of a snail or slug.

Even if these objects (and, in the case of the head at least, we cannot really be sure that it is an object) are what they might seem to be, they give us no real clues as to the nature of the creature. It is easy to underestimate the hostility to life of the environment that is Loch Ness.

**RIGHT** **A 1950s joke postcard from Inverness, Scotland. The creature in Loch Ness certainly hasn't done any harm to the tourist trade in the north of Scotland.**

*Captured!! Arrival of the Loch Ness Monster at Inverness!*

The loch is about 250m (820ft) deep, only the uppermost 40m (130ft) or so of which tolerates normal marine creatures. Below that there is vritually no animal life at all, and very little other life, in water whose temperature varies hardly at all throughout the year from a chilly 5.5°C (42°F). Thus any denizen of the depths would have to be a plankton-eater; but plankton is much more plentiful in the surface regions, so we would expect to see the monster there quite frequently. If the creature were a mammal like a seal it would be frequently seen on the surface; besides, seals breed on land. Turning to the other major divisions of the animal kingdom, we note that reptiles would, so far as we know, be unable to withstand the cold and amphibians would, again, either be more frequently observed or would long since have migrated in search of a more hospitable environment. These conclusions leave us with only the fishes, and here there may be a possibility. Eels and a number of other types dwell on the bottoms of bodies of water, rising towards the surface to feed, which they do primarily at night. A huge, unknown species of eel might well fit the specifications, and there are a few other piscine candidates. Yet fish of these types are not noted for their nimble wits, and hence it seems very curious that we haven't yet caught any or come across any dead ones.

## FACT OR FANTASY?

One might be tempted to dismiss the Loch Ness Monster as the purest of fantasies were it not for the fact that similar tales are told of numerous other inland bodies of water around the world. Some of these legends may be imitative – we skip with reasonable confidence away from

BELOW **Photograph taken at Loch Ness by Jennifer Bruce in 1982.**

Morag, the monster reputed to dwell in Scotland's Loch Morar – or, conversely, the Loch Ness legend may itself be imitative of others. Irish lake monsters are mentioned from as early as the 10th century, and sightings have been recorded up to the present day, sometimes in startlingly small bodies of water, such as Lough Fadda, in County Galway, which is barely 2.5km (1½mi) long. Here, in 1954, a librarian called Georgina Carberry was on a fishing expedition with three friends when they saw across the water what looked from the distance like someone out for a swim. It was only as the creature came closer to the shore where they were standing that they realized that this initial guess was wrong. The creature had a long neck, raised high above the water, at the end of which was a toothed and gaping mouth; the body of the monster seems to have been eel-like although, as it lost interest in them and turned away, they saw it had a bifurcate tail. In 1965 an investigator, Captain Lionel Leslie, detonated an explosive charge near to where Carberry and her friends had seen the monster. The explosion seems to have startled something large and living, for there was a great deal of threshing offshore as a result, but it was impossible to make out any details, and an attempt two years later to catch the beast by setting a net across the lough met with no success. Similar netting exercises performed on a few of the other Irish loughs – monsters have been reported from many more than just a handful – have likewise yielded nothing.

A couple of persistent features of these Irish monsters are interesting for a quite unrelated reason. First, the creatures' heads are frequently said to resemble those of horses (the beasts are often called horse-eels), and the creatures themselves are not restricted to the water, but can comfortably disport themselves on shore. The erect ears of a horse could well remind us of the two horns observed on the "head" photographed by Rines in Loch Ness; but, much more significantly, the two characteristics of the Irish creatures are strongly reminiscent of the tales told in western Scotland about kelpies. It seems very possible either that the Scots, migrating from Ireland to Scotland during the 5th and 6th centuries, brought their monster-stories with them or, since the two regions are separated by only a narrow passage of sea, that the monsters did indeed have a range that extended over both but that the Scottish branch has since largely died out.

# NORTH AMERICAN LAKE MONSTER

Speculations about the Scottish-Irish monsters' common heritage in no way help to account for the diverse reports from North America of lake monsters – about 100 lakes and rivers in the USA and Canada are credited with having such beasts. By far the best known of these is Ogopogo, which is said to inhabit Okanagan Lake in British Columbia. The creature's name can be dated precisely to 1926, when W. H. Brimblecombe sang at a lunch party in Kelowna, on the lake's shore, a song he had composed about the monster based on an original UK nonsense song

**LEFT** **A model of Ogopogo on display at Kelowna, British Columbia.**

featuring a half-earwig/half-snail called Ogopogo. The creature itself had been observed since long before then, being known to the pre-Columbian Amerindian population as N'ha-a-itk, a name which means "lake monster" or "lake demon". According to most accounts, Ogopogo's head is horse-like, like those of the Irish monsters. Okanagan Lake is much like Loch Ness in many respects, although a little larger and colder than its Scottish counterpart: certainly a creature that found one lake conducive to a pleasant existence would be quite content in the other.

## ACCOUNTS OF OGOPOGO

The Amerindians of the region apparently accepted the existence of the creature as a fact of life, rowing their canoes to its supposed home in a cave near the lake's Squally Point in order to leave food there to appease the creature. An early report by one of the invading Whites came in 1890, when a certain Captain Thomas Shorts claimed that he had seen, from the steamer he was plying on the lake, a finned creature about 5m (16ft) long and with a head like that of a ram; however, this was at a time when North American newspapers were regularly being fed hoax "wowee!" stories by their far-flung correspondents, and presumably also Captain Shorts, as skipper of a steamer, had some interest in the number of tourists who might come to Okanagan Lake, so we cannot place too much reliance on his account. Other reports came every two or three years until 1926, which seems to have been a bumper year for Ogopogo sightings. In November of that year the monster was observed by between 50 and 60 people who had come to the lakeside for a baptism. A few months before some hoaxers built a model; it is said that some of the people who believed they were looking at the model discovered to their horror, as the thing suddenly dived, that in fact it was the real monster – a tale rather too good to be true. In December the *Vancouver Star* gave great prominence to a report that Okanagan Lake had iced up and that Ogopogo had been discovered dead on the surface of the ice. On discovering that the lake was unfrozen and Ogopogo nowhere to be seen, the newspaper had to print a retraction, the secondary headline for which bears repeating: "Investigation fails to support theory of death."

Few sightings of the beast were reported during the war years, but in the late 1940s and 1950s they picked up again. In July 1959 the editor of the *Vernon Advertiser*, R. H. (Dick) Millar, and his wife were out on the lake when they saw the creature. According to Millar's own account:

> It was travelling around fifteen to seventeen miles an hour (24–27kph). The head was about nine inches (23cm) above the water. The head was definitely snakelike, with a blunt nose . . . We watched for about three minutes, as Ogie did not appear to like the boat coming on him broadside, (he) very gracefully reduced the five humps which were so plainly visible, lowered his head and gradually submerged. At no time was the tail visible . . . This sea serpent glides gracefully in a smooth motion (without snakelike undulations sideways). This would lead one to believe that in between the humps it possibly has some type of fin, which it works together or possibly individually to control direction.

Like the Loch Ness Monster, Ogopogo has been captured on film, although considerable controversy surrounds the short movie clip concerned, and the man who shot it, Arthur Folden, a mill worker from Case, British Columbia, was sufficiently concerned about the matter first

**RIGHT** **A view across Okanagan Lake, British Columbia, towards Squally Point and Ogopogo Island. The lake is the home of by far the best known of the North American water monsters.**

OGOPOGO'S HOME

Before the unimaginative, practical whiteman came, the fearsome lake monster, N'ha-a-itk, was well known to the primitive, superstitious Indians. His home was believed to be a cave at Squally Point, and small animals were carried in the canoes to appease the serpent.

Ogopogo still is seen each year – but now by white men!

DEPARTMENT OF
RECREATION & CONSERVATION

of all to be reluctant about showing it in public and, later, after all the hubbub, even about being interviewed. He and his wife were driving home alongside the lake after a day's outing when they saw something moving in the water. There was still the tag end left in his 8mm cine camera, equipped with telephoto lens, of the film on which he had been recording the jollities of the outing, and Folden used this up in short bursts to capture the animal whenever it showed itself above the surface. However, Folden was wary of publicity; although he showed the results to acquaintances, he forbade them to spread the word. Finally, however, his brother-in-law persuaded him that he should permit the film a public airing; by then, however, the film was not in very good shape and the image was at best indistinct. The suggestion was made that Folden was a hoaxer, and he retired from the public arena. From the film it could be estimated that the creature was about 1m (3ft 3in) in diameter and about 18m (60ft) long.

In 1976 a certain Ed Fletcher, from Vancouver, was with a party of friends when they spotted Ogopogo. The creature remained in view for some hours as they pursued it backwards and forwards along the shore-line. Fletcher took a set of five photographs of the monster; it has to be admitted that what is claimed to be a several-humped monster looks a lot more like a standing-wave effect, but Fletcher and his friends were adamant that they had seen the creature's head, which had two erect ears. It does seem curious that Fletcher, in all that while, took only five photographs; it doesn't seem to have been a case of him having only five left in the camera, because then, surely, he'd have shot them all off pretty quickly, not knowing that the monster was obligingly going to remain in view for so very long.

## OTHER SIGHTINGS

Once Ogopogo had made its first massive inroads into the popular consciousness, reports came in of similar monster legends and sightings from countless other North American lakes. New credence was given to accounts from the 1820s to the 1890s of a beast seen numerous times in Norway's Lake Storsjön; there have been rare further sightings up until the present day, but these may well be sheer wish-fulfilment, since the Lake Storsjön monster has, like Ogopogo, become a tourist attraction. A little closer to home there was considerable excitement in Newport, Arkansas, about the beast which had been seen numerous times in the White River nearby since first being reported in detail in 1937 by a plantation owner named Bramlett Bateman, who later did a good trade charging tourists 25¢ per time to come onto his riverside land to see if

**ABOVE** **The runestone on Frösön Island in Lake Storsjön, Sweden. The lake is the home of a much-reported monster researched around the turn of the century by Dr Petter Olsson. It is said that the runestone will bind the monster in the lake until such time as someone deciphers its inscription.**

**ABOVE  A model of the monster reported to have been sighted in Japan's Lake Ikeda. Inevitably, the monster has been nicknamed Issie.**

they could see the "thing".

Returning to Canada, we discover monsters whose relationship to Ogopogo may be betrayed by their names. There had been various reports during the 19th century of a monster in Simcoe Lake, Ontario, and after a particularly detailed witnessing in 1952 the creature became Igopogo – also Kempenfelt Kelly, for the bay in which it is supposed to dwell. After Kempenfelt Bay was accidentally flooded with raw sewage in 1980 the monster was soon discovered near Cook's Bay.

## MANIPOGO

*Of significant interest of the aquatic monsters is Manipogo, the denizen of Lake Manitoba. This was first sighted in 1908 (unless we take account of Amerindian legends, which always miraculously appear whenever a "new" monster hits the headlines). There were various other reports, climaxing in 1957, when a number of detailed accounts appeared, including one that mentioned that the monster's cry was like a "goods train's whistle". This was enough for the provincial government to send in an investigative team, which found nothing. In 1960 Dr John A. MacLeod of the Department of Zoology, University of Manitoba, mounted a brief scientific expedition in search of Manipogo, which seems to have responded by displaying itself promiscuously that summer to anyone save the scientists – indeed, on one occasion 17 people witnessed not one but three monsters: a mummy, daddy and baby Manipogo having a family outing. In 1962 two fishermen, John Konefell and Richard Vincent, not only had a good sighting (of a solitary creature) but were able to take a photograph. Here again one is impressed by the modesty of the observers' claims, and so it is tempting to suspect that, whatever Konefell and Vincent saw, it was certainly something.*

Despite all these reports, and countless others, North America's only serious rival to Ogopogo itself is probably the monster of Lake Champlain, which lies along the boundary between Vermont and New York State, with part of its length just inside Quebec. According to modern mythology, Champ, as the beast is known, was first seen by the French explorer Samuel de Champlain (1567–1635) in 1609, when he discovered not only the lake but also more than he had bargained for; in fact, de Champlain was talking of a monster reputed to frequent the St Lawrence estuary. The earliest authenticated accounts date from 1819, when a number of settlers independently claimed to have seen the creature. These went largely unremarked until 1871, when the passengers of a lake steamer, the *Curlew*, reported seeing a large creature with a neck rearing high above the water; this was not the first but it was certainly the most compelling of a cluster of sightings that year. Through the later years of the 19th century there were further sightings, some of them quite detailed, and in 1899 there was even a report of the creature being seen dragging itself up on shore. The level of observations continued unchanged through much of the 20th century. Joseph M. Zarzynski, who has mounted numerous scientific expeditions to the lake since 1975, has speculated that the increasing use of the lake by human beings may be driving the creatures either into timorous hiding or completely out of existence, and various conservation measures have been taken. In 1977 Sandra Mansi and her fiancé saw a creature on the lake; luckily she had her pocket camera with her, and she was able to take a photograph before Champ sank from view. She didn't release the photograph until some years later, in 1981, when Champ fever was spreading not just nationally but internationally; by then, unfortunately, she had lost the negative, so detailed analysis of the photograph was impossible, although on the basis of the print alone it was possible to rule out trickery. This is not to say that the photograph's subject is the giant-eel-like Champ: it is possible that Mansi and her fiancé were themselves victims of a hoax (although they swear the creature was in motion) or that, as Roy P. Mackal has proposed, what looks like a long neck and a smallish head is in fact the tail-fin of a submerging whale; Mackal suspects that a supposedly extinct type of whale, the zeuglodon, is at the core of most lake-monster stories.

## FINDINGS OF AQUATIC MONSTERS

What must be evident from all these accounts of aquatic monsters is the surprising degree of correlation between all the various descriptions. If we bear in mind that different witnesses were observing a moving, twisting object at different times and in different places, and that none of them could set to work with a tape-measure, we can justify saying that the monsters they saw were all of similar size. The high-held head on its long neck and the upright ears or horns recur again and again (and ears could certainly be sometimes flat against the head, thus explaining their nonappearance in some cases). It is thus reasonable to suppose that, if these monsters do in fact exist, they are all of the same species (or at least genus); the infernally difficult problem is trying to determine what species (or genus) that might be – or even which phylum of the animal kingdom, as we saw in connection with the Loch Ness Monster. This has led some people – the Forteans John Michell and Robert Rickard in *Phenomena*, for example – to propose that the creatures are not straightforward animals at all but human-derived entities with roughly the same physical status as ghosts, belonging to subjective rather than objective reality. The theory has its facets of interest, but leads to a dead end. A more down-to-earth version of the hypothesis might be that a "model of expectations" was early established through reports of sea-serpents and bolstered through the original descriptions of sightings like those at Loch Ness; subsequently witnesses of things that could not easily be emphasized may have "read back" the evidence of their senses until it conformed with the "acceptable" model. Similar comments may of course be applied if the creatures do indeed have a more humdrum status in good, old-fashioned objective reality: they may be of different morphologies and habits, but witnesses nevertheless unconsciously tailor their observations to conform with the model of expectations. In which case there are any number of candidates presented to us by the crypto-zoologists, from manatees to crocodiles to plesiosaurs to Mackal's zeuglodon and beyond. The problem is compounded by the fact that not all of the lakes from which reports have come are freshwater: some are salt.

# SEA-MONSTERS

Are there any clues to be gained from carrying the investigation through to salty waters? Here the difficulties of evaluating reports are much more considerable because, for obvious reasons, any single observation in the middle of the ocean can never be properly correlated against any other: the chances of two groups of observers at different times catching sight of the same individual creature are in practical terms zero. For this reason I do not propose to go into a long recital of accounts of sea-serpents, giant octopi and giant squids (the likely source of stories about the kraken), since the reports are all much of a muchness, and most of them date back to a more credulous age. Not all, however: one dates from 1966, when Chay Blyth and John Ridgway were rowing across the Atlantic. It was night and Blyth was taking his turn asleep when Ridgway had an unusual experience:

> I looked out into the water and suddenly saw the writhing, twisting shape of a great creature. It was outlined by the phosphorescence in the sea as if a string of neon lights were hanging from it. It was an enormous size, some 35 or more feet [10.7 + m] long, and it came towards me quite fast. I must have watched it for some 10 seconds. It headed straight at me and headed right beneath me. I stopped rowing.

the Age of Reptiles, looking like crocodiles except for the thing fact that they are 15–20m (50–65ft) long.

Sea creatures sighted near the shore, and thus presumably inhabitants of littoral waters, are much more easily assessed than their deeper-water counterparts. A couple of creatures have been observed off the coasts of Cornwall and Wales in the UK. The more famous is the Cornish beast, Morgawr – meaning "sea giant" – which presented itself a number of times during 1975–6. In February 1976, at Rosemullion Head, near Falmouth, a woman was able to take a couple of photographs of it, and the only reason that has ever been found to doubt the evidence of these is that the woman herself still insists on anonymity. Although the pictures are not of very good photographic quality, they are, if genuine, more revealing than virtually any other taken of a water monster. The portion of the monster that we can see above the waves is 5–6m (15–18ft) long; the body is bulky yet flexible, so that the back could well look "humpy" if only shallowly above the water-level; the neck is long and gracefully curving, and the head is small.

A somewhat similar (although reportedly rather smaller) monster was the one seen in 1975 by a party of schoolgirls walking on the beach of Cardigan Bay, in Wales. Their art teacher was able to do a sort of Identikit portrait of the beast based on their descriptions; later, when he showed it to a crew of local fishermen who had reported a monster nearby, they recognized it immediately – although we should not be too bullish about this corroboration, because the likelihood of "reading back" having played a part is obviously very high. And from halfway around the globe, between British Columbia and Vancouver Island, in the Strait of Georgia, there have come reports of a further similar – although this time, at 14m (45ft) long, much bigger – creature, these sightings dating from as long ago as 1932 and continuing, albeit infrequently, to the present day. The British Columbian creature is known locally as Caddy, a dimunitive of Cadborosaurus.

ABOVE **Photograph of Morgawr the Cornish sea monster taken by a witness – "Mary F." – during February 1976.**

# CAPTAIN EADES'S MERMAID

As with most fakes, dead "mermaids" were concocted from bits of other animals – or worse. In the 18th century a Dr John Parsons (1705–70) discovered that a small "mermaid" being exhibited in London was in part composed of a human foetus. The most famous of all these monstrosities was brought to London in 1822 by a Bostonian called Captain Eades; it had been shown around the world for a few years before that, and reports from abroad ensured that its arrival would be a cause célèbre. Eades himself seems to have been convinced of the authenticity of his grisly possession; certainly he showed no inhibitions in requesting Sir Everard Home, President of the Royal College of Surgeons, to examine the object. Home sent William Clift, Curator of the Hunterian Museum, in his stead. Clift reported:

> The cranium appears evidently to belong to an orang-outang of
> full growth, the teeth, and probably the jaws, do not belong to
> the cranium, but from the size and length of the canine teeth,
> they appear to be those of a large baboon. The scalp is thinly
> and partially covered with dark-coloured hair, which is glossy
> like that of an orang-outang. The skin covering the face has a
> singularly loose and shrivelled appearance and on a very close
> inspection, it appears to have been artificially joined to the skin
> of the head across the eyes and the upper part of the nose. The
> projections in lieu of ears, are composed of folds in the same
> piece of skin of which the face is formed. The eyes appear to
> have been distended by some means, so as to have kept very
> nearly the natural form, and there is a faint appearance as
> though the cornea had been painted to represent the pupil and iris.

Clift's report went on to analyse the rest of the "mermaid" in similar detail. Tufts of black hair had been fixed into each nostril. The fingernails of the original ape had been replaced by artifices in some substance which he couldn't identify. Beneath the breasts, which seemed to have been padded, there was a deep fold which camouflaged the join marks of the upper and lower parts of the body. This lower part was composed of an entire fish except for its head, the skin of the fish's back being overlaid onto the orang-utan's back while still fresh. The fish's body had been "fleshed out" by the insertion of a tube of "some firm substance, similar to paper or pasteboard". Another observer, Edward Donovan, suggests that the exhibit looked rather like the frozen moment in time when a large fish realizes that the ape it has been trying to swallow whole is too large for it. The "mermaid's" facial expression was one of great anguish, as if the creature had died in agony. If we are to believe the autobiography of P. T. Barnum (1810–91), it was this very same specimen that came into his hands in 1842 and, as the "Feejee Mermaid", started the turnstiles lucratively a-ticking.

A drawing of a mermaid that was put on display (for a fee, of course) at the St Bartholomew Fair in 1825; it had been brought to London in 1822 by the Bostonian Captain Eades. Its components were identified by Sir Everard Home as having come from an ape and a fish.

## MAMMALS OR REPTILES

If indeed these sea-monsters are of the same ilk as their lake counterparts, we are presented yet again with a dilemma noted in connection with lake monsters should we wish to regard them as fishes – giant eels, for example: they seem equally happy in salt and fresh water. If not figments of the imagination or some sort of psychic reification, then, they must be mammals or, just possibly, reptiles.

Certainly mammals can reach the sort of dimensions we're concerned with. Leaving aside the whales for obvious morphological and behavioural reasons, we still find some other mammals. Notable among these are the giant sea cows first described in detail by the naturalist Georg Wilhelm Steller (1709–46), a survivor of the shipwreck that accounted for Admiral Vitus Bering (1680–1741) on what is now called Bering Island. During the winter that the survivors had to spend there they preyed upon the great coastal sea creatures which, to their own misfortune, seemed quite unafraid of human beings. These animals were giant sea cows, related to the dugong or manatee, and according to Steller could reach lengths of nearly 11m (36ft). Once the expedition had returned home the area was inundated by hunters and trappers who likewise slaughtered the pathetically amiable creatures, and very swiftly, by 1768, the giant sea cows were seemingly extinct. However, there have been in the region a number of sightings since then of large marine animals that seem very much like the giant sea cows, and so it is possible that there is a viable population still in existence. Of course, it would be too much to expect that these Arctic creatures might have a range extending well into temperate latitudes, but it is feasible that some of the more northerly lake monsters might represent isolated populations of them. However, their friendly-seeming demeanour and their need to

**RIGHT A young Steller's sea cow, as seen by the naturalist and explorer Georg Wilhelm Steller during his enforced winter on Bering Island.**

breathe at the surface would presumably make them highly visible animals, and so we would expect sightings to be much more frequent than in fact they are. However, their very existence – unknown except for the 27 short years between their discovery and their presumed extinction – indicates how possible it might be for there to be other large marine mammals, of more reclusive habits, inhabiting northerly waters and still surviving because they are undiscovered by human beings except in rare sightings.

# MERMAIDS

Manatees and dugongs are more often mentioned – along with seals – as the root of stories about mermaids; Steller himself made the connection. Any of these creatures can display a surprising degree of "humanity" in their sorrowful facial expressions, and it is possible that after months at sea those doleful eyes could blind a man to an animal's other physiological features. According to an unpublished letter sent back by a serviceman to a UK magazine during the campaign to recapture the Falkland Islands from Argentina in 1982, even penguins were discovered by himself and his fellows to display unexpected allure, so it is not too hard to imagine sailors being drawn to the sympathetic-seeming dugong. Yet this would hardly seem to account for the lovingly detailed descriptions of mermaids that have come down to us. Moreover, far from all sightings of mermaids have been by lust-maddened seamen. For example, around the end of the 19th century a teacher called William Munro observed on the bleak shore of Caithness, Scotland, a brown-haired beauty perched atop a rock. A dozen years later he wrote about it to *The Times*:

> The head was covered with hair of the colour above-mentioned and shaded on the crown, the forehead round, the face plump, the cheeks ruddy, the eyes blue, the mouth and lips of natural form resembling those of a man; the teeth I could not discover, as the mouth was shut; the breasts and abdomen, the arms and fingers of the size of a full-grown body of the human species, the fingers, from

ABOVE **The canine head of the mermaid depicted in this early illustration certainly suggests a connection between the beautiful sea-woman of legend and, rather more prosaically, known marine mammals such as the seal or the dugong.**

the action in which the hands were employed, did not appear to be webbed, but as to this I am not positive. It remained on the rock three or four minutes after I observed it, and was exercised during that period in combing its hair, which was long and thick, and of which it appeared proud . . .

The detail of the mermaid combing her hair is enough to arouse suspicion about the rest of Munro's account, yet very obviously he had seen *something* that he was convinced had human form; moreover, he claimed that others in the locality had seen the same or a similar creature around the same period, so we cannot dismiss his claim with quite the abruptness we might wish. Nor do we know quite what to make of the following, which is from the year 1608 in the log of the explorer Henry Hudson (d.1611):

ABOVE **A mermaid depicted in a 12th-century cathedral in Eire. Note the detail of the comb and mirror.**

> This morning one of our company, looking overboard, saw a mermaid, and calling up some of the company to see her, one more came up, and by this time she had come close to the ship's side, looking earnestly on the men; a little after, a sea came and overturned her. From the navel upward her back and breasts were like a woman's (as they that saw her), her body as big as one of us; her skin was very white; and long hair hanging down behind of the colour black; in her going down they saw her tail, which was like the tail of a porpoise, and speckled like a mackerel.

Hudson himself was clearly a trifle sceptical about this report, as evidenced by his cautious parenthesis. Somewhat uneasily we must conclude that the creature was in fact a seal or something of the kind.

In folklore mermaids do not customarily deploy the charm and cuteness typified by the depiction in, say, the 1989 Disney feature *The Little Mermaid*. Instead they have many of the characteristics of the succubus or the *lamia* being sexually alluring but cold, cruel and potentially body – and soul-destroying to any man who should succumb to their charms. Here we have a parallel with the shapeshifting silkie of Scottish folklore, which was both very sinister indeed and definitely, in the tales themselves, identified with seals. There are also connections with the legends of, respectively, valkyries, the Morrigan (Morgan le Fay) and the sirens, not to mention (again) the *lamia*, for the mermaid according to some accounts was a fallen angel that lured men to her by means of her heavenly singing and then, capable as she was of eating only living flesh, ate her fill of the luckless swain. Only a little less gloomily, there was also a superstition that catching sight of a mermaid foretold the observer's imminent death from drowning; this presumably was based on the notion that the mermaid had permitted herself to be seen because she was attracted by the luckless seaman and would take the first opportunity to carry him away to the rich submarine kingdom of the merfolk.

Yet the identification of mermaids with seals and/or sea cows seems irresistible. Certainly legends about seal maidens and mermaids are very often interchangeable, turning up in one place with a skin-shedding seal as protagonist and in another with a mermaid performing exactly the same function in the story. Moreover, a strong thread of folklore describes the seal as being the ever-present guardian of the mermaid, which would suggest that even the most credulous observers were prepared to admit that, whenever they saw a mermaid, there were also lots of seals around.

As early as 1829 the Scottish naturalist George Johnston (1797–1855) was producing compelling proof that such a creature as a mermaid – at least, one built according to the popular conception – was impossible. He pointed out, for example, that if mermaids had lungs this must mean they had to come to the surface frequently in order to breathe: were this the case, they would be quite commonly seen. Mermaids were presumed to have voices but, if they were fish-like, they would not be able to hear anything, so their voices would be useless for communication, and their bewitchingly beautiful siren-songs would go to waste. Also, a fish of human size would require more than just a tail-fin to propel it along its way; besides the lack of any fin to give supportive movements to the torso and head would mean that the mermaid's "rest mode" would be vertical and upside-down.

Despite sporadic sightings reported well into the 20th century – in 1947 in the Hebridean island of Muck, in the 1950s in northern Scotland, in 1957 in the South Seas, in the early 1960s off the Isle of Man (one of the best sightings being by the Mayoress of Peel, no less), in 1978 in the Philippines, and many others – we must still conclude that the mermaid is no more than a being of myth, born at least in part from distorted observations of sirenians such as seals and dugongs. Another contributor to the myth may have been ancient tales of fish-gods, which crop up in mythologies from many parts of the world although rarely in such a convincing fashion as in the accounts of Oannes. Or perhaps even the fish-gods had their origins in observations of seals. Or perhaps genuine eyewitness accounts of the Apkallu were passed down through the ages by word of mouth until they became a potent background element of our collective folk tradition, ready to be sparked back into existence by later misobservations of seals. Or perhaps . . .

**ABOVE** A romanticized 19th-century French view of the mermaid. What is truly astonishing about this picture is the way the seamen seem so matter-of-fact about the encounter.

# BIBLIOGRAPHY

BORD, Janet and Colin, essays from *The Unexplained* assembled in *Creatures from Elsewhere* (ed Peter Brookesmith), London, Orbis, 1984

BOWEN, Charles (ed), *The Humanoids*, Chicago, Regnery, 1969, rev 1974

BRUNVAND, Jan Harold, *Curses! Broiled Again!*, New York, W. W. Norton, 1989

CLUTE, John, and NICHOLLS, Peter (ed), *The Encyclopedia of Science Fiction* (2nd edn), Little, Brown, London, 1992

COHEN, Daniel, *The Encyclopedia of Monsters*, Waltham Abbey, Fraser Stewart, 1991 (reprint of 1982 edn)

COSTELLO, Peter, *The Magic Zoo: The Natural History of Fabulous Animals*, London, Sphere, 1979

COSTELLO, Peter, *Searching for Lake Monsters*, New York, Coward, McCann & Geoghegan, 1974

COSTELLO, Peter, essays from *The Unexplained* assembled in *Creatures from Elsewhere*, ed Peter Brookesmith, London, Orbis, 1984

CROSSLEY-HOLLAND, Kevin (ed), *Folk-Tales of the British Isles*, London, The Folio Society, 1985

DALE, Rodney, *The Tumour in the Whale: A Collection of Modern Myths*, London, Universal, 1978

DANCE, Peter, *Animal Fakes and Frauds*, Maidenhead, Sampson Low, 1976

DAVIDSON, John-Paul, "A Portrait of the Yeti as an Ancient Ape", BBC *Wildlife*, October 1988

DRAKE, W. Raymond, *Gods or Spacemen*, London, Spearman, 1964

FARSON, Daniel, and HALL, Angus, *Mysterious Monsters*, London, Bloomsbury Books, 1991

FRANCIS, Di, *Cat Country: The Quest for the British Big Cat*, Newton Abbot, David & Charles, 1983

GAUTE, J. H., and ODELL, Robin, *The Murderers' Who's Who*, London, Harrap, 1979

GOOCH, Stan, *Cities of Dreams*, London, Rider, 1989

GOSS, Michael, *The Evidence for Phantom Hitch-hikers*, Wellingborough, Aquarian Press, 1984

GOULD, Stephen Jay, *Hen's Teeth and Horse's Toes*, New York, W. W. Norton, 1983

GRANT, John, *A Directory of Discarded Ideas*, Sevenoaks, Ashgrove, 1981

GRANT, John, *Dreamers: A Geography of Dreamland*, Bath, Ashgrove, 1984

GRANT, John, *Great Mysteries*, London, Apple Press, 1988

GRANT, John, *An Introduction to Viking Mythology*, London, Apple Press, 1990

HARRISON, Fred, *Brady and Hindley: Genesis of the Moors Murders*, Bath, Ashgrove, 1986

HEUVELMANS, Bernard, *In the Wake of the Sea-Serpents*, London, Rupert Hart-Davis, 1968 (trans)

HEUVELMANS, Bernard, *On the Track of Unknown Animals*, London, Rupert Hart-Davis, 1958 (trans)

HOUSEHOLD, Geoffrey A. (ed), *The Devil's Footprints*, Exeter, Devon Books, 1985

HURWOOD, Bernhardt J., *Terror by Night*, New York, Lander, 1963

KRUPP, E. C. (ed), *In Search of Ancient Astronomies*, London, Chatto & Windus, 1980; rev edn London, Penguin, 1984

LANDSBURG, Alan, *In Search of Myths and Monsters*, London, Corgi, 1977

LANGFORD, David, *An Account of a Meeting with Denizens of Another World, 1871* (as by William Robert Loosley), Newton Abbot, David & Charles, 1979

LANGFORD, David, "Me and Whitley and the Continuum", "Secrets of UFO Research" and "MJ-Balls!" in *Sqlodion #2*, April 1990

LESLIE, Desmond, and ADAMSKI, George, *Flying Saucers Have Landed*, London, Futura, 1977 (rev edn)

MACKAL, Roy P. *The Monsters of Loch Ness*, London, Futura, 1976

MACKAL, Roy P. *Searching for Hidden Animals*, New York, Doubleday, 1980

MASTERS, Anthony, *The Natural History of the Vampire*, St Albans, Rupert Hart-Davis, 1972

MENZEL, Donald H., and TAVES, Ernest H., *The UFO Enigma: The Definitive Explanation of the UFO Phenomenon*, Garden City (NJ), Doubleday, 1977

MICHELL, John, and RICKARD, Robert J. M., *Phenomena: A Book of Wonders*, New York, Pantheon, 1977

MILLAR, Ronald, *The Piltdown Men*, London, Gollancz, 1972

NAPIER, John, *Bigfoot: The Yeti and Sasquatch in Myth and Reality*, London, Cape, 1972

PATERSON, Neil, "The Mark of the Kelpie", *The Scots Magazine*, January 1991

RANDLES, Jenny, *Mind Monsters: Invaders from Inner Space?*, Wellingborough, Aquarian Press, 1990

RANDLES, Jenny, essays from *The Unexplained* assembd in *The Alien World*, ed Peter Brookesmith, London, Orbis, 1984

RANDLES, Jenny, and WHETNALL, Paul, *Alien Contact: Window on Another World*, Sudbury, Spearman, 1981

RIDPATH, Ian, *Messages from the Stars*, London, Fontana, 1978

SACHS, Margaret, *The UFO Encyclopedia*, London, Corgi, 1981

SANDERSON, Ivan T., *Abominable Snowmen: Legend Come to Life*, Philadelphia and New York, Chilton, 1961

SHKLOVSKII, I. S., and SAGAN, Carl, *Intelligent Life in the Universe*, New York, Holden-Day, 1966

SHUKER, Karl P. N., *Mystery Cats of the World*, London, Hale, 1989

SHULMAN, Sandra, *Nightmare*, Newton Abbot, David & Charles, 1979

SUMMERS, Montague, *The Vampire: His Kith and Kin*, London, Kegan Paul, Trench, Trubner & Co., 1928

TANNAHILL, Reay, *Flesh and Blood: A History of the Cannibal Complex*, London, Hamish Hamilton, 1975

TCHERNINE, Odette, *The Snowman and Company*, Lond, Hale, 1961

TCHERNINE, Odette, *The Yeti*, London, Spearman, 1970

TEMPLE, Robert K. G., *The Sirius Mystery*, London, Sidgwick & Jackson, 1976

TOMBAZI, N. A., *Account of a Photographic Expedition to the Southern Glaciers of Kanqchenjunga in the Sikkim Himalaya*, Bombay, Maxwell, 1925

WADDELL, L. A., *Among The Himalayas*, London, Constable, 1899

WATSON, Lyall, *Lifetide: A Biology of the Unconscious*, London, Hodder & Stoughton, 1979

WILSON, Colin, *A Criminal History of Mankind*, London, Granada, 1984

WILSON, Colin, *Written in Blood: A History of Forensic Detection*, Wellingborough, Equation, 1989

WILSON, Colin, and GRANT, John (eds), *The Directory of Possibilities*, Exeter, Webb & Bower, 1981

WILSON, Colin, and WILSON, Damon, *The Encyclopedia of Unsolved Mysteries*, Chicago, Contemporary Books, 1988

# INDEX

## PICTURE CREDITS

British Film Institute: p9 (top). Black Museum: p79. C M Dixon: pp46, 86 (bottom), 94, 99, 124. Jean Loup Charmet: pp74, 75, 77, 83. Fortean Picture Library: pp2, 8, 9, 10, 11, 13, 14, 19, 21, 23, 25, 26, 27, 28, 29, 30, 31, 32, 33, 34, 35, 36, 37, 38, 39, 40, 41, 42, 43, 44, 51, 52, 55, 56, 58, 59, 60, 62, 63, 64, 66, 67, 68, 69, 70, 71, 72, 78, 88, 91, 95, 96, 101, 105, 107, 108, 109, 111, 112, 113, 114, 119 (bottom), 121, 122, 123, 125. Tom Frost: p17. Dougal Haston: p15. Images Colour Library: pp54, 61, 65, 80, 81, 86 (top), 98, 102, 117. National Film Archive: pp118, 119 (top). Wide World Photos: p82.